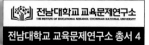
전남대학교 교육문제연구소
THE INSTITUTE OF EDUCATIONAL RESEARCH, CHONNAM NATIONAL UNIVERSITY
전남대학교 교육문제연구소 총서 4

A Handbook for Educational Research and Academic Writing: From Idea to Reporting Your Research

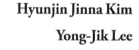
Hyunjin Jinna Kim

Yong-Jik Lee

PARKYOUNG
publishing&company

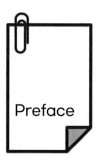

Preface

Our decision to write this book, "A Handbook for Educational Research and Academic Writing: From Idea to Reporting Your Research," did not happen overnight. As educators, researchers, and scholars, we understand the intricate process one needs to undertake in the journey of pursing knowledge creation and effective communication. This handbook was created out of our collective passion for fostering excellence in educational research and academic writing.

After completing our Master's and Ph.D. degrees in the United States, we met and worked with many graduate students working toward their degrees. Dr. Yong−Jik Lee (hereafter Lee) returned to South Korea and has been working on many international publications. Dr. Hyunjin Jinna Kim (hereafter Kim) remained in the United States, conducting educational research with various departments and experts in different fields. The first few years immediately after earning our Ph.D., we lived with the memory of and under the shadow of our dissertation and research. We observed graduate students struggling to master academic writing conventions while enduring the pressure of completing their degree programs and balancing all the expectations of being an emerging scholar.

Working with those new to educational research taught us the importance of uncovering rigorous research processes in education. Lee noticed that some graduate students' thesis and dissertation presentations had complex diagrams and pictures with a 'fancy' analysis method. These were interesting research topics, but students could not answer some basic questions when he asked about the theoretical backgrounds. The students' research projects lacked theoretical foundations and were designed superficially to claim something with eye−catching visuals and analysis tools. Kim collaborated with undergraduate student research projects and non−education experts to realize that the rigorous educational research steps and processes are complex and not well−established. We also came to the realization that academic writing as a genre and educational research as a discipline are both new cultural experiences no matter where you came from or what linguistic and cultural backgrounds you have.

The landscape of education is ever−evolving, demanding a robust understanding of research methodologies and effective communication skills. Whether you are a graduate student embarking on your first research project or an early−career academic navigating the complexities of academic culture and scholarly writing, we hope this handbook will be a supportive companion on the road from conceptualization to the reporting stage of your research.

Based on a few years of observation and working with undergraduate students, graduate students, and researchers, we noticed a gap in educational research and academic writing. We began to reflect on our research experiences in the U.S. and realized that writing a handbook to support those involved in the writing and scholarly community in education can be immensely helpful. We found the necessity of addressing the cultural and knowledge gap every emerging scholar or novice writer experiences and making those implicit cultural norms rather explicit.

Our aim is to provide a comprehensive guide that not only demystifies the research and academic writing process but also empowers you to articulate your ideas with clarity and impact. Each chapter is constructed to address specific stages of educational research and academic writing. We intend to offer practice insights, actionable advice, and illustrative examples throughout this handbook. From noticing an educational problem to refining your research question, from crafting a captivating introduction to selecting appropriate research methods, from effectively presenting your results to carefully formulating your discussion, this handbook provides guidance at every step of your research and academic writing journey. We wrote this handbook to provide a sound research process and guidance for completing your essential academic writing piece. We hope this book offers proper yet practical research writing skills to support your research endeavor.

This handbook was specifically designed to achieve the following purposes.

- To highlight the valuable and advantageous experiences beyond obtaining a graduate degree.

- To transform the landscape of educational research and academic writing practices.

- To outline the appropriate research steps and directions for producing high−quality research.

- To emphasize the importance of conducting ethical and rigorous research.

- To reiterate the real purpose behind academic writing and shift perspectives from recognizing research methodology as a tool to creating and presenting innovative research.

- To guide and support those entering the realm of academic writing and educational research to present high−quality academic papers and become international researchers and scholars in the future.

While rooted in the principles of academic rigor, we recognize the need for flexibility and inclusivity and acknowledge that there is no one−size−fits−all approach to educational research and academic writing. The authors' shared experiences, lessons learned, and practical tips are intended to resonate with you, the reader, as you embark on your own scholarly journey. Consider this handbook not only as a guidebook but as a conversation—a dialogue between mentors and mentees. Use it as a resource to enhance your knowledge, advance your skills, overcome challenges, and, above all, find inspiration in the transformation of educational research.

May this handbook accompany you from the first innovative research idea to the moment you proudly wrap up reporting your research findings. We extend our heartfelt wishes for a fruitful and fulfilling academic journey.

Happy researching and writing!

Hyunjin Jinna Kim, Ph.D.
Yong–jik Lee, Ph.D.

Table of
Contents

Part I. Academic Writing and Educational Research

Part II Step-by-step Guidelines: From Idea to Reporting

Part III. Furthering Research and Academic Writing

List of
Figures

PART

I

Academic Writing and Educational Research

What is Academic Writing?

 Opening Questions

- How would you define academic writing?
- What are the features and characteristics of academic writing?
- How could developing academic writing skills advance your personal or professional purposes and goals?

 In this chapter, you will···

- Define and identify the elements and characteristics of academic writing.
- Explain the meaning of academic writing relevant to your purposes and goals.
- Evaluate your purposes and goals through the lens of academic writing.

Academic writing is, on its own, a writing genre that encompasses various formats, such as essays, reports, dissertations, articles, and more. Each form adheres to stylistic and structural norms that underscore clarity, precision, and a principled approach to delivering knowledge and ideas. It weaves comprehensive research, systematic analysis, and expression, forging a pathway for scholarly dialogue and discovery.

Characteristics and Features of Academic Writing

Formality and Tone: Academic writing necessitates a formal and objective tone, mitigating personal biases and abstaining from everyday usage. For instance, instead of employing informal language, including the use of contractions, the constant use of the pronoun "I", an academic researcher would utilize word choices that reflect formality. Furthermore, passive voice is often preferred to denote an impartial stance, such as stating "the experiment was conducted" rather than "I experimented."

Structure and Organization: Scholarly texts should exhibit a coherent structure, typically encompassing an introduction, body, and conclusion. In essays, the typical "five−paragraph" structure is known to reflect a balanced allocation of one paragraph introduction, three paragraphs body, and one paragraph conclusion. Each section must intertwine with the next, ensuring a logical progression of ideas. For example, a research paper may be organized by presenting the research question first, followed by methodology, results, discussion, and conclusion. Within each section or paragraph, the structure is maintained to include an introduction, body, and conclusion to some extent.

Evidence−Based: Grounding your assertions in empirical evidence and relevant literature is pivotal. For instance, when asserting a relationship between variables, one might reference a study stating, "According to Smith (2020), a significant correlation was identified between..." This may seem straightforward when you are quoting another scholar's work, but trying to apply this principle in your own research writing referring to your data can pose a challenge. Any piece of academic writing is inherently argumentative. You are trying to make an assertion, an argument, or a claim. The key is to support every single assertion with evidence.

Precision and Clarity: Adopting precise language and ensuring clarity are important aspects to maintain. A sentence like "The drug was somewhat effective" is less desirable than "The drug reduced symptoms by 30%." Also, keep in mind that academic writing pieces are often quite lengthy, which increases the chances of being one−sided. Suppose you are listening to someone's speech for five minutes as opposed to one hour. There is no room for Q&A, and you wrote down all the questions you had during the speech. Which list of questions would be longer? The list of questions from a five−minute speech or the one−hour speech? Most likely, your list of questions is longer after listening to the one−hour speech. Academic writing is a rather one−sided communication because it is inherently lengthier than other forms of writing and often has no or limited opportunities to interact with your readers. This means you need to be clear and precise so there is no room for confusion or questions.

Citation and Referencing: Crediting sources and adhering to citation styles, such as APA, MLA, or Chicago, exemplifies academic integrity and provides a roadmap for academic readers to explore the underlying research. Citation styles are often particular to certain disciplines and fields of research. It is often expected that scholars and academic writers adhere to the very details of citation conventions. If not, certain criticism or judgment follow, as much as a writer leaving a misspelled document uncorrected. Citation styles are treated similarly to grammatical rules. In academic writing, mistakes and errors in citation conventions are sadly often interpreted as the writer's incompetence. It is important for writers to know the citation styles in their discipline, forward and backward, with extensive attention to detail.

Diversity in Academic Writing Styles

While academic writing is a genre of its own, there are a range of styles in academic writing. It is common to incorporate many of these styles in a single academic writing piece.

Analytical Writing: This style necessitates examining and interpreting various elements of a topic or concept. For example, an analytical paper on climate change might dissect its causes, impacts, and potential mitigation strategies, scrutinizing each component meticulously.

Persuasive Writing: Often deployed in argumentative essays or proposals, persuasive writing seeks to persuade the reader towards a particular viewpoint. For instance, a piece advocating for renewable energy adoption would provide evidence to substantiate the benefits and feasibility of such technologies.

Descriptive Writing: Descriptive writing can delineate a process, phenomenon, or research method, ensuring readers understand the necessary knowledge pertaining to a specific topic.

Critical Writing: Based on evaluative and analytical components, critical writing can involve a theory, methodology, or findings, necessitating a thorough examination and contextualization of the subject matter.

As mentioned earlier, most academic writing pieces incorporate all the styles introduced above. An artful incorporation of these styles reflects the writer's skills and the researcher's knowledge of the subject matter.

Academic Writing: Challenges and Solutions

Novice researchers, such as graduate students, often grapple with synthesizing information, maintaining objectivity, and adhering to stylistic norms of academic writing. Below are some possible solutions to tackle such challenges.

- *Reading:* Conducting rigorous reading of academic texts, known as a literature review, to internalize pertinent writing styles and strategies is necessary.

- *Reflective writing:* As mentioned earlier, academic writing is more or less a one–sided conversation. In real–life face–to–face conversations, even without the opportunity to exchange questions and answers, you can pick up non–verbal cues and use them as feedback to elaborate, repeat, or strategize to engage the audience. In academic writing, you need to be a reflective writer, looking back on what you wrote and addressing confusion.

- *Writing and rewriting:* Along with reflective writing, embrace the practice of writing and rewriting. Think about the great speeches you heard that last for decades. These were not composed in a few seconds on the spot. They were carefully crafted, practiced, and revised for a very long time. To write an impactful and well–structured piece, it is crucial to remember that the piece you are writing is not the final draft.

- *Applying tools:* Utilizing writing resources, such as seeking feedback from peers and mentors to refine skills effectiveness, and employing technological tools, such as citation generators and grammar checkers, enhances the accuracy and coherence of research papers.

With its characteristic features and diverse styles, academic writing facilitates scholarly discourse, knowledge dissemination, and intellectual exploration. Navigating its complexities involves understanding and internalizing its inherent norms and adapting writing strategies to align with the targeted communication goals. Through continuous practice, feedback, and resource utilization, you can develop a repertoire of academic writing strategies, contributing substantively to the vibrant tapestry of scholarly dialogues.

Academic Writing Skills for Personal and Professional Development

Academic writing holds a unique position. It is precise, structured, and evidence–based, making it a crucial skill set for various purposes. Developing proficiency in academic writing augments our capabilities within an educational context and provides us with tools to benefit our personal and professional lives.

Credibility and Authority: At its core, academic writing revolves around the presentation of researched facts, logic, and critical thinking. As such, the ability to write academically bestows the writer an aura of credibility and authority. As an emerging scholar, this contributes to shaping your scholarly identity and boosting your reputation as a researcher.

Clarity and Precision: One of the hallmarks of academic writing is its emphasis on clarity. By prioritizing concise language, clear structure, and logical progression, one learns to convey complex ideas easily. This skill is invaluable in professional settings where precise communication can differentiate between success and failure in drafting contracts, writing memos, or developing marketing materials. Clear and precise communication also promotes inclusivity in a team environment where implicit norms are made clear to everyone.

Critical Thinking and Analysis: Beyond the surface, academic writing fosters an analytical mindset. By habitually questioning sources, seeking diverse viewpoints, and evaluating evidence, one hones the skill of critical thinking. This analytical process enhances personal decision–making and makes one a more astute professional, capable of making well–informed choices and offering deeper insights. Critical thinking skills developed through academic writing allow one to problematize societal issues, seeking solutions and innovative approaches to make changes.

Lifelong Learning: The research inherent to academic writing promotes a culture of continual learning. Needless to say, delving into the world of academic writing and research is a humbling experience. As one delves into literature reviews or data analysis, the habit of seeking knowledge gets entrenched. This curiosity can translate into personal growth as one remains open to new ideas and experiences. Professionally, it keeps individuals updated, adaptable, and at the forefront of their fields.

Transferable Skills: Academic writing is about more than just putting words on paper. It involves research, time management, organization, and adherence to guidelines and standards. These are all transferable skills that could be applied anywhere from personal to professional lives. For instance, the research skills honed while writing a thesis can be invaluable when investigating market trends or competitor analysis in a business scenario. The project and time management skills developed from academic writing may become useful to avoid procrastination and organize one's personal life.

In conclusion, academic writing, often perceived narrowly as a tool for scholars, has wide–reaching implications. Its principles, when internalized, can enhance personal discernment and professional competence. In a world inundated with information, critically evaluating, structuring, and communicating knowledge is not just an asset but a necessity.

Reflection Questions

▸ What types of academic writing are more or less familiar to you?

▸ What did you learn about academic writing? How does this inform your plans to develop academic writing skills?

▸ How could developing academic writing skills advance your personal and professional endeavors? Consider the following aspects to establish your personal and professional goals:

Personal goals	Professional goals
Having work-life balance: • *Time management* • *Planning*	*Publishing in a top-tier journal:* • *Persistence* • *Goal setting*

Time management Analytical skills Problem-solving Decision-making Classifying Coordinating Creative thinking Goal setting	Organization Critical thinking Communication Researching Evaluating skills Persistence Planning Project management
Academic writing skills	

Conducting Educational Research

Opening Questions

- What do you know about conducting educational research?
- How does educational research differ from other research approaches?
- What are the gaps in your understanding of educational research and the necessary procedures?

In this chapter, you will···

- Chart approaches to conducting educational research.
- Outline the knowledge and skills needed to conduct research.

Educational research serves as a conduit through which educators, policymakers, and stakeholders glean insights into educational phenomena, pedagogical practices, and student outcomes. By navigating through varied methodologies, ethical considerations, and analytical practices, researchers explore pathways toward richer learning experiences and equitable opportunities for student success in education.

Methodological Approaches in Educational Research

Common methodological approaches in educational research range from quantitative to qualitative and mixed−method research. Each approach is dependent on the researcher's research philosophy, research questions, and aims. Each approach also carries its own advantages and disadvantages.

QUANTITATIVE RESEARCH

Quantitative research focuses on phenomena through numerical data and statistical analysis. Often employed to identify patterns, relationships, or differences among groups, it underpins the researcher's assertions with empirical and numerical data. For instance, a quantitative study can explore the correlation between students' attendance and academic performance, utilizing statistical analyses to discern patterns or causality.

QUALITATIVE RESEARCH

Qualitative research focuses on experiences, perceptions, and contextual interpretations. It seeks to unpack the underlying meanings of educational phenomena by exploring methods like interviews, observations, or content analysis. An example can involve investigating teachers' experiences and challenges during remote learning through in−depth interviews to illuminate the realities and challenges encountered.

MIXED-METHOD RESEARCH

Mixed−methods research synergizes quantitative and qualitative approaches to enhance their collective strengths. A study exploring the efficacy of an educational intervention can employ quantitative methods to gauge improvements in test scores while concurrently implementing qualitative methods to explore students' and educators' experiences and perceptions of the intervention.

Data Collection in Educational Research

Numerous data collection methods are available to investigate your research questions. Although we are introducing a few common data collection methods, bear in mind that this book is not intended to delve deep into research methodologies. Rather, we intended to outline a few commonly known basic methods to help carry the discussions throughout this book.

Aligning methodology and research questions: Consider a study aiming to examine the impacts of socio−economic status (SES) on remote learning during pandemic−induced school closures. A quantitative approach can entail administering surveys to data related to SES indicators, technological access, and academic outcomes, ensuring a robust, quantifiable exploration of the research question.

Selecting and implementing data collection tools: The selection and implementation of data collection tools must be planned, ensuring fidelity to the research design and practicality within the logistical confines.

- Surveys and questionnaires: Quantitative research can employ surveys to gather large−scale data, such as gauging student engagement levels across various learning platforms.
- Interviews and focus groups: Qualitative research can utilize interviews or focus groups to delve into participants' experiences and perceptions, offering rich and nuanced insights.
- Observations: Researchers can engage in observational data collection, exploring, for instance, classroom dynamics, teaching practices, or student engagement.

Ensuring data quality and relevancy: Ensuring that the data you collected are high—quality and relevant to your research questions allows your findings to be robust and meaningful.

- Pilot testing: Before full—scale data collection, pilot testing ensures that tools such as surveys or interview protocols are clear and relevant and elicit the desired data.

- Continuous monitoring: Throughout the data collection, continuous monitoring ensures that the process adheres to the outlined plans and that adjustments can be made if unforeseen challenges arise.

- Triangulation of data: Triangulation of data, often utilized in qualitative research, involves collecting multiple data sources using multiple methods. This allows a collection of different perspectives in order to address and answer your research questions.

Analyzing and Interpreting Data in Educational Research

After data collection, sufficient time will be spent on data analysis. As mentioned in the previous section, we do not plan to offer comprehensive data analysis strategies. Rather, we aim to outline the different stages involved in conducting educational research in order to provide steps and strategies for academic writing in the subsequent chapters.

Data analysis strategies: Data analysis must be executed precisely and rigorously, ensuring the results are valid, reliable, and substantiated. In a quantitative study exploring the impacts of class size on learner outcomes, statistical analyses must be selected and accurately performed to ensure the findings are credible and defensible. In qualitative study, various data analysis strategies are available (e.g., thematic, dialogic, critical analyses, etc.), often determined by your research philosophy, theoretical perspectives, and the type of data you collected.

Ensuring validity and reliability: Ensuring the research's results are valid (accurately reflecting the researched phenomenon) and reliable (consistent in measurements and outcomes) is crucial. Utilizing robust instruments, meticulously performing analyses, and verifying findings enhances the research's credibility. In qualitative research, validity and reliability are often established through trustworthiness.

Dissemination and Knowledge Mobilization

Once analyzed and substantiated, results must be disseminated through relevant channels, such as academic journals, conferences, or other digital platforms. This process enables the knowledge to be mobilized and applied within relevant contexts and communities, thereby enriching practice and policy.

Conducting educational research requires an in−depth navigation through methodological innovations, ethical considerations, and analytical rigor. By adhering to research principles, respecting participants' rights and dignity, and ensuring robust and credible analyses, educational researchers illuminate insights that can enhance educational practices, inform policy, and enrich learning experiences across diverse educational contexts. Honing your academic writing skills impacts and contributes to the dissemination of knowledge. Thus, we hope to provide comprehensive guidelines to help you throughout the journey of conducting educational research and reporting your research.

The Authors' Reflection

Depending on the program, Ph.D. students must take certain credit hours of coursework related to research methodologies. In U.S. higher education, students might be asked to take at least 12 credits of research methodology courses. In some cases, this is required at the Master's level as well, especially if the field of study is designed to proceed to a Ph.D. degree program following a Master's degree program. For some graduate students in their Master's program, there are also opportunities to take these courses if the student is determined to pursue a Ph.D. degree program. The following is a list of research methodology courses you can expect to see in graduate course catalogs.

- Foundation of Research Methods
- Qualitative Research: Data Collection
- Qualitative Research: Data Analysis
- Introduction to Quantitative Research Methods
- Quantitative Research Design and Methods
- Advanced Quantitative Research Methods
- Survey Design
- Meta-analysis
- Statistics
- Academic Writing
- Mixed Methods Research

Unfortunately, graduate students in Korean higher education may not have access to a variety of research methodology courses as observed in U.S. higher education institutions. In other words, graduate students and beginning scholars must search and study research methodologies in-depth before diving into independent research.

Regardless of the courses offered by the program, it is critical to obtain extensive knowledge of the research methodology you intend to employ in your research. It is also equally important to keep yourself up to date with different research methodologies, as these certainly change and advance over time.

The following are a few references to dip your toe into the foundation of research methodology:

Creswell, J. W. (2013). *Research design: Qualitative, quantitative, and mixed methods approaches.* SAGE Publications.

Creswell, J. W. (2015). *A concise introduction to mixed methods research.* SAGE Publications.

Creswell, J. W., & Poth, C. N. (2018). *Qualitative inquiry and research design: Choosing among five approaches.* SAGE Publications.

Denzin, N. K., & Lincoln, Y. S. (2017). *The SAGE handbook of qualitative research*

(5th ed.) SAGE Publications.

Harvard Catalyst (2022). *Mixed methods research*. Havard College. https://catalyst.harvard.edu/community−engagement/mmr/

Hoy, W. K., & Adams, C. M. (2016). *Quantitative research in education: A primer*. SAGE Publications.

SAGE Research Methods (2022). *Methods map*. SAGE Publications. https://methods.sagepub.com/methods−map

Reflection Questions

▶ Compare and contrast your understanding of research in general and educational research. How are they similar and different?

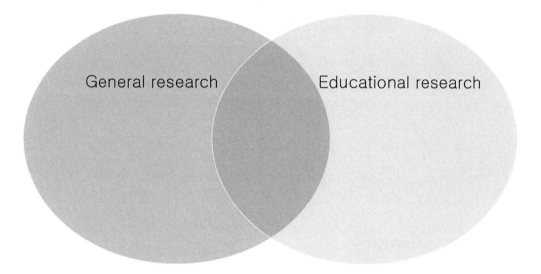

General research   Educational research

▶ What are some specific plans you can make to advance your knowledge in conducting educational research?

Situating Academic Writing in Educational Research

Opening Questions

- What are the skill sets needed in academic writing? What about conducting educational research?
- What role does academic writing play in educational research?

In this chapter, you will···

- Demonstrate your understanding of educational research.
- Identify the role of academic writing in educational research.
- Construct an understanding of academic writing to advance educational research.

Academic writing and educational research intertwine in a symbiotic relationship, where the former becomes the vehicle through which research is communicated, critiqued, and built upon. A potent academic writing framework amplifies the integrity of research findings and becomes a critical tool for knowledge dissemination and discourse within the academic community.

The Essence of Academic Writing in Research

What role does academic writing take in your research? How does developing your academic writing skills inform your research and vice versa?

Conveying complexity with clarity: Educational research often delves into complex, multifaceted societal phenomena. Consider a study exploring the diverse factors influencing student engagement in online learning, where data can encompass socio−economic variables, technological access, cognitive load, and motivational factors. In order to conduct this study, your academic writing skills must intertwine the numerous threads into a coherent, accessible narrative, maintaining simplicity without sacrificing complexity. As you develop academic writing skills, you are simultaneously advancing your ability to convey complex concepts with clarity.

The impetus of precision: Precision in academic writing can help researchers avoid ambiguity and misinterpretation. A study quantifying an educational intervention's impacts must clearly define variables, explicate methodologies, and delineate findings, ensuring that the resultant narrative is accurate and replicable. Again, in order to communicate precision, you ought to practice precision in your research procedures. Attention to precision in academic writing and research, thus, compliments each other.

Navigating through the Structural Facets

The structural facets of academic writing also encourage you to develop the necessary skill sets as a researcher. As we walk through the structure of academic writing, you will notice how academic writing skills are interwoven into conducting research.

The abstract and introduction: Academic writing often begins with an abstract and a comprehensive introduction, situating the study within the broader context. For instance, research exploring flipped classrooms can be conducted by exploring prevailing educational paradigms, identifying gaps, and articulating the research inquiries being pursued. This is a critical step in the stage of establishing your problem as a researcher, which is when you need to think about the specific contexts and gaps in knowledge concerning the problem you intend to address. The abstract and introduction call for this process, which we will discuss further in Chapter 8.

An exposition of rigor through the methodology: The methodology section is not merely an exposition of the research process but a testament to the researcher's rigor and knowledge. Consider a qualitative study exploring teacher perceptions, where the methodology must detail the data collection strategies (e.g., interviews, focus groups) and articulate the rationale, ensuring the reader can discern the alignment with the research philosophy and questions. Research methodology, an essential component in academic writing, asks the researcher to study and grapple with their philosophy, perspective, and research aims.

A balanced discourse in findings and discussion: Navigating through the findings and discussion necessitates a balanced approach, ensuring findings are presented impartially. In contrast, the discussion critically engages with the data, situating it within the wider educational landscape. As a researcher constructs a narrative to effective report the findings and provide critical interpretations and claims in the discussion, analytical and critical thinking processes are necessary. These processes, in turn, enhance your academic rigor and in−depth reflection.

Ethical Narratives in Academic Writing

The process of academic writing also calls for ethical research conduct through the practices of being transparent, objective, and evaluated. Below, we outline a few aspects of academic writing that inform researcher's ethics.

Transparency and honesty: Upholding an ethical narrative involves ensuring that limitations are discussed and findings are presented honestly. If the researcher encounters unexpected hurdles, such as data inconsistencies or methodological limitations, these must be transparently communicated within the academic writing piece, upholding the integrity of the discourse. Furthermore, an ethical use of sources expected in academic writing encourages transparency and honesty throughout the research process.

Engaging with peer review: A dialogic process of peer reviewing, inherent in academic writing, provides an avenue for researchers' ethical conduct in the research and writing journey.

- Receptivity to critique: Once submitted to academic journals, your research enters the realm of peer review—to be critiqued and evaluated by peers. Thus, academic writing must be robust enough to withstand scrutiny and flexible enough to be adaptable in the light of constructive criticism.

- Iterative refinement: Engaging with peer reviews often necessitates revisiting academic writing, refining arguments, justifications, or clarifying ambiguities, underscoring the iterative nature of academic writing within the research process. This process encourages the researcher to be ethical, both in their research conduct and writing.

Academic Writing as a Tool for Impact and Change

Well−articulated research can inform policy, shape practices, and inspire further research. For instance, a study exploring the efficacy of technology−enhanced learning can influence educational policymakers, prompting an exploration into infrastructural investments or pedagogical training for educators. Thus, academic writing becomes a catalyst for research from the academic realm into the practical and policy domains. As we emphasized earlier in Chapter 2, dissemination of knowledge is critical in research, and academic writing plays a key role in dissemination. We will discuss this further in Chapter 15 as well.

Academic writing is also an intricate art form, balancing clarity with complexity, precision with accessibility, and robustness with adaptability. In situating academic writing within educational research, graduate students and emerging scholars should navigate a journey that extends from the initial conception of ideas to their communication, critique, and potential implementation, contributing to the vibrant, dynamic tapestry of educational discourse and development. Your refined academic writing piece can be the first step to making an impact and real change in the field.

Promoting Your Educational Research through Academic Writing

Advancing educational research through academic writing involves synthesizing rigorous research methods with clear, structured writing. Here is how it can be achieved:

- *Stay of current literature*: Regular engagement with recent academic publications keeps you updated on the latest methodologies, debates, and gaps in the field. This can inspire new research questions and methodologies.

- *Adopt a clear structure*: A well−organized paper, with clearly demarcated sections for introduction, literature review, methodology, findings, and conclusions, makes your research more accessible and persuasive.

- *Seek feedback before publication*: Sharing drafts with peers, mentors, or experts in the field can provide invaluable feedback. They might offer insights, critiques, or perspectives yet to be considered.

- *Engage with a broader audience*: Apart from academic journals, consider writing for magazines, blogs, or newspapers that cater to educators or the general public. This enhances your visibility and tests the applicability and relevance of your research. It is also an opportunity to broaden your adaptive academic writing skills to tailor to the audience.

- *Collaborate*: Consider co−authoring papers with other researchers. Such collaborations can offer fresh perspectives, divide the workload, and expand the reach of your research. Furthermore, you are given an opportunity to be exposed to diverse academic writing styles, which diversifies your language use.

- *Continuous Skill Enhancement:* Attend workshops or courses on academic writing. The better your writing skills, the more effectively you can communicate your research.

In summary, while educational research seeks to understand and enhance education, academic writing serves as its voice, ensuring that the insights derived reach the right ears and have the desired impact. Together, they drive the evolution of educational paradigms, shaping the learners of today and tomorrow. We will take another deep dive into this topic again in Chapter 14.

▸ What does it mean to use academic writing to advance your educational research?

▸ Identify the skills and knowledge you would like to advance in academic writing and educational research.

Research Procedures

 Opening Questions

- If you were asked to conduct educational research, what steps would you take? At which point do you get stuck?
- Where should you start if you are planning to conduct a new educational research project?

In this chapter, you will⋯

- Summarize procedures for conducting educational research.
- Plan approaches and steps for your research project.

Initiating research endeavors necessitates planning and adherence to a structured procedure, ensuring the study's validity, reliability, and ethical soundness. The procedures involve everything from initial conception to methodology implementation, data analysis, and finally, the reporting of findings. We will outline typical research procedures with practical examples and insights to help you navigate the complex process of research and academic writing.

Conception of Research: Ideation and Framing

Academic research begins with identifying a pertinent research question or problem substantiated and framed within the existing literature.

- *Literature Review*: An ethical exploration of extant literature enlightens the researcher regarding previous explorations, existing gaps, and potential trajectories. For instance, examining studies on online learning may reveal a scarcity in exploring educators' experiences, thereby illuminating a potential research avenue. This is a rather complex and long process, and we will dive deeper into the nuts and bolts in Chapter 8.
- *Framing Research Questions*: Informed by the literature, researchers construct their research questions, ensuring they are both relevant and novel. An example research question could be: "What are the experiences and challenges educators encounter during remote teaching?"

Once the research questions are established, depending on the types of data to be collected, an IRB review process will take place before the researcher can take any further action. In conjunction with or after the IRB review process (see Chapter 5 for more details), some researchers find it helpful to create a research timeline (see Figure 1). This is not a requirement; however, it is a good practice as creating a research timeline is often necessary in collaborative research projects or research grant applications. It is notable to recognize that research projects commonly take more or over a year from start to finish. A basic research timeline is also helpful to include in your IRB review documents, providing a rough timeline to the reviewers about how long the data might be kept.

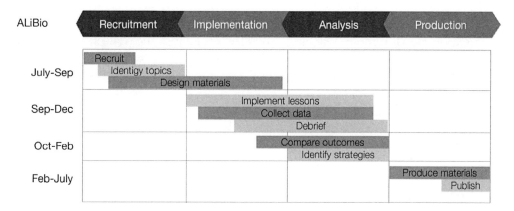

Figure 1. Sample Research Timeline

Research Design and Methodology

As we outline the basic steps in conducting research, keep in mind that there is a long process of going back and forth between each step and various complications involved in each step. Part II of this book intends to tackle and demystify each step.

RESEARCH DESIGN & METHODOLOGY

The research design and methodology act as the blueprint, guiding data collection and analysis.

- *Choosing a research design*: Depending on the research question(s) and research philosophy, a researcher may choose a qualitative, quantitative, or mixed—methods research design. A study exploring educators' experiences can opt for a qualitative design, enabling an in—depth exploration of their narratives.

- *Selecting research methods*: Researchers must select methods that align with their design and questions. Continuing the example above, semi—structured interviews might be selected to garner rich, detailed data regarding educators' experiences.

- *Sampling strategies*: Identifying and selecting participants/sample is pivotal, ensuring the sample is representative and pertinent. Purposive sampling, for instance, might be employed to ensure participating educators have experienced remote teaching, thereby enriching the data's relevance and applicability.

DATA COLLECTION & MANAGEMENT

- *Executing data collection*: Implementing the selected methods involves ensuring the data's reliability and validity. In executing interviews, for instance, consistency in questioning and a conducive environment ensures robust data collection. A detailed data collection plan is essential not only to receive an IRB review approval but also to conduct rigorous and ethical research.
- *Data management*: Employing strategies to securely and systematically manage data safeguards its integrity and ensures its availability for analysis. Employing secure storage and systematic filing allows the data to be both safe and accessible. Data management plans are also one of the documents you are expected to submit for IRB review.

DATA ANALYSIS & INTERPRETATION

Data analysis transforms the raw data into meaningful insights, addressing the research questions.

- *Analyzing data*: Employing suitable analytical strategies enables the data to be meaningfully interpreted. Qualitative data from interviews, for example, might be analyzed employing thematic analysis, distilling the data into pertinent themes and patterns.
- *Interpreting findings*: Interpreting the findings involves situating them within the larger research context, considering their implications, relevance, and potential applications.

Reporting and Dissemination of Findings

Once analyzed and interpreted, research findings are reported, disseminated, and contributing to the scholarly community and potentially informing practice and policy.

- *Selecting Platforms*: Researchers must identify suitable platforms, such as academic journals, conferences, or digital mediums. This allows valuable research findings to reach relevant audiences.

- *Communicating Findings*: Effectively communicating findings involves considering the audience and tailoring the reporting of the research to be accessible, understandable, and engaging to the respective audiences.

Critical decisions, ethical considerations, and methodological rigor enrich your academic writing and research journey from conception to dissemination. By navigating this path with attention to each stage's demands and complexities, you can contribute meaningfully to the knowledge exchange, offering insights that may illuminate understandings, inform practice, and shape future explorations.

The Authors' Reflection

When the authors were in Ph.D. programs in the U.S., we were invited to join research projects with our academic advisors. As research assistants, we learned how to conduct rigorous research. Below are some research steps we learned without explicit guidelines available at our disposal.

1. *Search relevant literature*: Review previous studies on the research topic— What studies were done before?

2. *Synthesize literature:* Organizing studies based on specific sub−topics

3. *Write a literature review*: Summarizing the literature—*What did previous studies find out?*

4. *Identify the gap in the literature or set a hypothesis*: Identifying what might be missing in the previous studies. What are the gaps in previous research? What results are expected if similar research is conducted again?

5. *Design the research study*: Establishing research design, data collection, and analysis methods and developing measurement tools if needed.

6. *Apply for Institutional Review Board (IRB) review*: Outlining the background,

purpose, and methodology of the research, especially for human subject research, to protect the researcher's and participants' rights.

7. *Collect data*: Beginning participant recruitment, receiving informed consent, or getting permission from the research site to collect data once IRB approves the study.

8. *Analyze data*: Reding, noting, running tests, or coding collected data based on the research design and methodology — sometimes, this happens simultaneously with data collection.

9. *Report results or findings*: Writing the research report, thesis, or dissertation.

We want to highlight that for graduate students, the experience of a research assistantship during graduate school is impactful and serves as a basis for conducting independent research in the future. Thus, we recommend actively seeking research opportunities. Communicating with an academic advisor is the first step to finding a new possibility to gain research experience. Although the role of a graduate research assistant can be overwhelming and challenging, it is an experience that will teach you more than some basic research knowledge.

 Reflection Questions

- ▸ What steps in conducting research seem more challenging to you than others? Why do you think it is?
- ▸ How much time would you allocate for each step in the research timeline? What are the specific tasks needed for each step? Try to create a rough timeline for your research project.

05

Research Ethics

- What is your understanding of research ethics?
- Why is it important to understand and abide by research ethics?
- What should a researcher consider of an ethical research conduct?

 In this chapter, you will⋯

- Discuss various aspects of research ethics and what it means to conduct ethical research.
- Evaluate situations that require ethical decision−making in research.

Understandings of Research Ethics

Research ethics pertain to the principles and guidelines researchers must adhere to when conducting any scholarly investigation. These ethics ensure research integrity, validity, and credibility while safeguarding participants' rights, dignity, and well−being and the broader community. Key tenets of research ethics include:

- *Informed consent*: Participants should be fully informed about the nature, purpose, and potential risks of the research, and they must voluntarily agree to participate.
- *Confidentiality*: Personal data and information shared by participants must be kept confidential unless explicit permission is given for disclosure.
- *Avoidance of harm*: Research should not pose physical, psychological, emotional, or social harm to participants.
- *Honesty and transparency*: Researchers should be truthful about their methods, findings, and potential conflicts of interest.
- *Objectivity*: Research should be free from bias, and personal or financial interests should not influence results.
- *Right to withdraw*: Participants should have the freedom to exit the research process at any point without facing repercussions.

Importance of Understanding and Abide by Research Ethics

There are several reasons why research ethics are emphasized. It is not as simple as, "Be honest because lying is bad." When we discuss research ethics in the context of research and academic writing, it is important to recognize the contribution research ethics make to the integrity of the research.

- *Credibility and validity*: Ethical research practices ensure the integrity of the research process. Abiding by ethical guidelines reinforces the reliability and validity of the research findings.
- *Trustworthiness*: Ethical research fosters trust among participants, stakeholders, and the broader academic community. When participants trust researchers,

they are more likely to engage genuinely, ensuring authentic data.

- *Protecting participants*: By prioritizing the well−being of participants, ethical research ensures that individuals are treated with respect and dignity, not merely as data sources.

- *Legal repercussions*: Many jurisdictions have laws governing research, especially involving human subjects. Ethical compliance helps researchers avoid legal complications.

- *Contributing to positive outcomes*: Ethical research can lead to beneficial societal outcomes. It ensures that results genuinely reflect studied phenomena, which can inform effective policy and interventions.

- *Professional Reputation*: Adherence to ethical standards enhances the reputation of researchers and their affiliated institutions, furthering their academic and professional endeavors.

Considerations for Ethical Research

To ensure the ethical integrity of the research, a researcher should consider the following:

- *Clear communication*: Ensure participants understand the research objectives, methods, and potential outcomes. Any technical jargon should be clarified.

- *Acquire informed consent*: Always obtain written consent (see Figure 2) after explaining the research thoroughly. Additional permissions might be needed for vulnerable groups (e.g., children).

- *Protect anonymity*: Use pseudonyms, codes, or other methods to shield participants' identities, especially when dealing with sensitive data.

- *Be transparent about funding*: Disclose the sources of research funding to highlight potential conflicts of interest.

- *Maintain data integrity*: Store data securely and do not manipulate or alter findings to fit preconceived notions or external pressures.

- *Regularly consult ethical guidelines*: Many academic institutions and professional organizations provide guidelines on ethical research. Regular

Informed Consent

Project Title:

Principal Investigator:

Department:

KEY INFORMATION: The information in this form is being used to seek your consent for a research study. Being in the study is voluntary; it is up to you.

The primary purpose of this study is ⋯

The study will last for the duration of the class (i.e., one semester).

During the study period, the researcher(s) will disseminate surveys to gather participants' non−identifiable demographic information and perceptions of ⋯ Interested participants will be invited to a focus group interview to expand the responses in their surveys.

RISKS: There are no other foreseeable risks of discomfort associated with your participation in this study.

BENEFITS: There is no direct benefit expected as a result of your being in this study.

PAYMENT TO YOU: There is no compensation for participating in this study.

CONFIDENTIALITY: Steps will be taken to help make sure that all the information gathered from you is kept confidential. When reporting findings, no personal identifiable information will be used, and the data will only be accessible to the research team members.

COSTS TO YOU: There are no financial costs associated with your participation in this study.

ALTERNATIVES: Your alternative to being in this study is to simply not participate. There will be no consequence if you decide not to participate or withdraw at any point during the study.

YOUR RIGHTS AS A RESEARCH SUBJECT: Your participation in this study is voluntary. You have the right to change your mind and leave the study at any time without giving any reason. Any new information that may make you change your mind about participating in this study will be provided. You will receive a copy of this consent form. You do not lose any of your legal rights by signing this consent form.

QUESTIONS ABOUT THE STUDY OR YOUR RIGHTS AS A RESEARCH SUBJECT: If you have any questions, concerns, or complaints about the study, you may contact ⋯ If you have any questions about your rights as a research subject, you may contact the research office at ⋯ If you sign below, it means that you have read (or have had it read to you) the information given in the form and you would like to be a volunteer in this study.

Subject Name (Printed)	Subject Signature	Date

Figure 2. Sample Informed Consent

consultation ensures you remain compliant.

- *Seek ethical approval*: Before beginning research, especially with human subjects, seek approval from an Institutional Review Board (IRB) or equivalent ethical review committee.

- *Stay updated*: Ethical standards can evolve. Attend workshops, seminars, or courses to stay updated on the latest in research ethics.

Acknowledge limitations: Every study has limitations. Being open about them ensures transparency and honesty.

- *Show respect*: Always treat participants respectfully, acknowledging their contributions and ensuring they feel valued and heard.

- In essence, the foundation of ethical research is respect — for the process, the participants, and the broader quest for knowledge. As researchers tread the path of discovery, these ethical guidelines serve as beacons, ensuring the journey benefits the individual and society.

Institutional Review Board (IRB)

The Institutional Review Board (IRB) is a group formed as an independent ethics committee at an institution to protect the ethical conduct of research, rights, and privacy. Any research that involves human subjects, such as educational research, is required to undergo an IRB review. Below are the common basic types/levels of IRB review.

Exempt: If the research activities involve no more than what is considered "minimal risk," the research will be categorized as an exempt review type. Minimal risk entails the probability or magnitude of physical or psychological harm people normally encounter in their daily lives. Educational research (e.g., activities such as surveys, interviews, educational assessments, public observations that do not include children or minors, analysis of previously collected information or data, etc.) often falls under the exempt category.

Expedited: To meet the requirements of an expedited review, the research does not pose greater than minimal risk, and there is no identification of the subjects. Examples of human subject data collected in expedited research are the collection of blood samples by finger stick, heel stick, or alike, the collection of biological specimens or other data through noninvasive procedures, etc. In educational research, data collected for non−research purposes, research employing survey, interview, oral history, focus group interviews to evaluate characteristics and behaviors, or collection of data from voice, video, digital, or image recordings will fall under the expedited review category.

Full: In educational research, it is very unlikely that the research will require a full review process. Research that involves more than minimal risk to human subjects requires a full review, meaning multiple review board members will assess the risk level of the research. If the research involves vulnerable populations (e.g., children, prisoners, elderly, pregnant women, or any other vulnerable populations), sensitive topics (e.g., illegal behaviors), clinical procedures that are rather invasive (e.g., drugs, devices, surgery procedures, etc.), or taking place where subjects may be at physical, psychological, or legal risk, a full board IRB meeting will take place.

What is IRB, and Why is it Important?

Without the IRB process, one can easily collect data and conduct research quickly with participants' verbal consent. However, when constructing research design, it could be a bigger problem if graduate students rush to collect data and conduct research without being fully prepared or knowledgeable about their research. Figure 3 below is a diagram illustrating the IRB process.

INFORMATION TYPICALLY PROVIDED FOR IRB

For educational studies, data sources typically involve surveys, interviews, classroom observation, writing pieces, student assessment products, including grades, etc. Documents required for a smooth IRB review process are the following:
- Subject/Participant recruitment strategies and products used for recruitment

outreach (e.g., a script for face−to−face visitation recruitment or an email template/flyer/URL for electronic recruitment).

- Specific strategies to render coercion (i.e., students feeling pressure to participate solely to please the teacher who holds the authority to determine student grades) if you are conducting research in your own classrooms. In the case of collecting data from your own classroom, these strategies need to be laid out step−by−step and provided along with the IRB review application.

IRB Review process

DESIGN	SUBMIT	RECEIVE	DECISION
Design research, develop measurements and/or data collection plan, secure faculty principle investigator.	Complete IRB request, review, and submit your request to the IRB office.	Wait to receive feedback from IRB reviewer. Talk to the IRB office for specific timeline.	Expect possible decisions from the IRB office: Approved Further review Revision required Full board
1	2	3	4

Figure 3. IRB Process

- Survey/Questionnaire sample if survey will be distributed.
- Sample interview questions if employed.
- Class observation protocols if employed.
- Informed consent form or script, depending on the level of review and identifiable data collected. The informed consent commonly provides plans to anonymize participants' identifiable data.
- Assent forms, especially if data are collected from college freshmen with an increased probability of including minors (under 17 years of age).
- Data collection, storage, and protection plans.

All data collected without the IRB process is invalidated in U.S. higher education. If data collection is not specified in the IRB documents, the data cannot be used for academic publication and reporting purposes.

▶ What did you learn about research ethics? What are aspects you have not considered or anticipated before?

▶ What are the actions you need to take in your specific research project in order to conduct ethical research?

PART

II

Step-by-step Guidelines
: From Idea to Reporting

06

Considerations Before Writing

 Opening Questions

- What are the few initial steps you would take to approach your research project and idea?
- How would you start the initial writing process once you have an idea formulated for your research?
- What contributes to a research writing piece with a strong organization?

 In this chapter, you will···

- Distinguish your intended research from the pre−existing body of research.
- Compare well−organized and poorly organized research writing.

Thesis writing, a piece of writing completed for advanced degree completion, may be considered the first step and the epitome of academic writing. Although graduate students typically engage in informal academic writing in advanced or graduate−level courses, one's ability to initiate, conduct, and execute an educational research project is often evaluated by thesis writing. In the U.S. higher education context, a thesis refers to the research and writing required to complete a Master's degree, while a dissertation refers to the research and writing produced to obtain a Ph.D. degree. In European higher education settings, both types of academic writing are commonly referred to as a thesis. For the purpose of this book, we will use the term 'thesis' to indicate both Master's thesis and Ph.D. dissertation writing: the two major products of academic writing in higher education.

In the initial phase of planning for thesis writing and academic writing at large, various factors need to be considered. Part II offers the structure and stages of the research process, starting with pinpointing a problem until you reach completion.

Considering the "Why"

Thesis and research writing distinguish themselves from the more basic types of academic writing, such as an essay or report, by their inherent nature. Through your research, you are embarking on a journey to identify a significant problem in your research field and, essentially, resolve that problem. As graduate students in higher education, your habit of posing essential and critical questions can become an important tool for you—not only as a writer but also as a researcher and knowledge creator. Below are some questions to guide your habit of questioning and problematizing.

- What are the major discussions and debates happening in my specific field? What is the nature of these discussions and debates? How many perspectives are there, and what are they about?
- What is exactly the problem? What is the cause of the problem? What is the

effect of the problem?

- As a researcher, which is of more value to me? Should I tackle the cause of the problem or the effect of the problem?
- Who and what am I trying to advance? Who will be my target audience?
- What am I trying to find out through my research?
- How will my research impact future researchers and contribute to the field?

Failing to address these critical questions before delving into thesis and research writing can result in weak, aimless, and unoriginal research that contributes minimally to the field and provides no purpose for the readers to read your written manuscript. The subsequent section provides an illustration of a poorly written thesis as an example.

- The research/thesis fails to provide a rationale or logical basis, thereby failing to persuade the audience.
- The research lacks support from a theoretical foundation or previous research.
- The research solely focuses on the relationship between variables, therefore causing confusion due to inadequate explanations of relevant theories.
- The results of the findings of the thesis lack proper support from previous studies.
- The organization of the thesis lacks cohesion to support the results or findings (refer to the following section for more details).
- Critical reflection and insights are absent in the discussion and conclusions sections.
- The research thesis inadequately explains the originality of the study. In essence, it merely replicates what others have previously done, offering no novel contribution to the field.

Organization of Your Research Writing

A meticulously structured thesis serves as a roadmap for developing a research project with a solid foundation. Additionally, cohesiveness aids researchers in comprehending the significance of your work within the field. What characterizes a well−organized thesis of high−quality? The following figure illustrates the basic structure needed for a quality thesis.

Corresponding to the basic structure, more details you need to consider in your thesis writing are outlined below.

ABSTRACT

Write your abstract last. A common mistake novice writers make is writing a thesis in the order it is commonly presented. The fact that an abstract is the first piece the audience will read does not mean it is the first piece an author should write. The abstract and oftentimes the introduction are best written last. There is no harm in writing down some outlines, but it is critical to refine your abstract and introduction once everything is written.

Invest in the writing of an abstract. Consider your abstract as a book cover. The abstract is the cover and face of your thesis. You should craft an abstract that is unique, attractive, succinct, and interesting.

Typically, the abstract contains a brief summary of the problem and the purpose of the research, an outline of the methodology, a few key findings/results, and the principal conclusion or implication.

INTRODUCTION

The initial chapter outlines the problem you plan to address, offering a background and problem statement. It is important to situate your problem in a larger context, henceforth establishing a territory. *Are you addressing the problem in a particular national context, field of study, or grade level?* This process contextualizes the problem for the audience and guides the researcher to problematize more at ease.

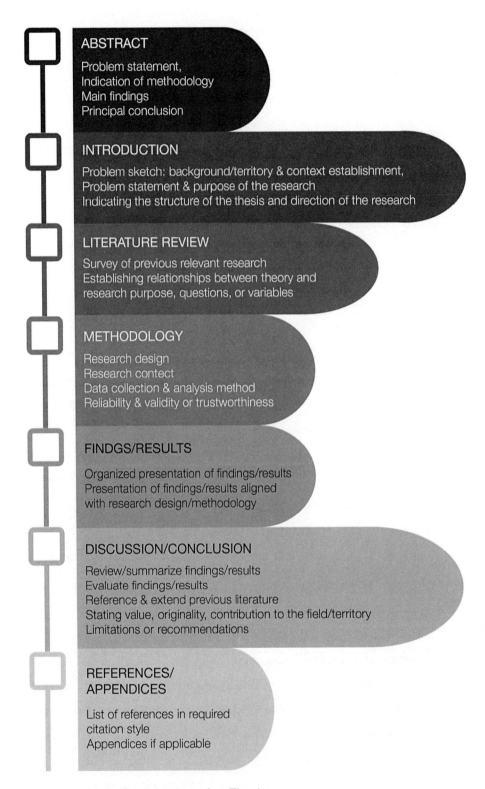

Figure 4. Basic Organization of a Thesis

This is the problem; thus, my research will solve the problem this way. A problem−solving approach helps introduce the research, clearly stating the problem and outlining the proposed solution.

The introduction logically conveys the research purpose, describes the problem backgrounds, illustrates the problem through multiple perspectives, outlines a brief summary of prior research and its attempts, provides counter arguments, and states research direction (purpose, research questions, and/or hypotheses).

LITERATURE REVIEW

The literature review section reviews previous research, presenting a clear outline of the theoretical background and framework. Consider the following questions before writing your literature review: *How did previous research address the problem, and did it approach the problem similarly or differently? How did previous studies frame their research, and what did or did not work? How is your research different, or why is your research important?*

The literature review needs to explain the connection between the theoretical background and the variables/research questions/research purpose. Justify your choice of the theoretical or conceptual framework in this section. In some cases, you may introduce new insights through a conceptual framework.

METHODOLOGY/RESEARCH DESIGN

It is crucial to dedicate enough time and space to clearly articulate the rationale for selecting the research design and methodology. The methodology and research design section includes a detailed explanation of the research design, context, study participants (subjects) or sampling methods, data collection process, and data analysis procedure. In quantitative research, the reliability and validity processes are explained, while in qualitative research, the trustworthiness is established.

FINDINGS/RESULTS

The findings or results are presented in an organized manner, tailored to the specific research design and methodology you proposed in the previous section. In the findings/results section, readability for the readers should be prioritized to ensure the findings are apparent to the readers rather than being overly focused on the author's perspective.

DISCUSSION/CONCLUSION

Emphasize the originality of your research: The discussion/conclusion section is sometimes combined or separated into two independent sections. The discussion section is a crucial part in your thesis or research writing that distinguishes your research from the existing literature. Specifically, the discussion section is where you explain how your research findings or results align or differ from and confirm or extend previous research.

Highlight the importance of your research: The discussion section is also a place for you to reiterate the relevance and importance of your research and findings. Circle back to the purpose/hypotheses/research questions as you highlight the critical contributions of your research findings/results. As you conclude, ensure that you are offering future directions and implications for research and/or practice.

An Undesirable Organization of a Research Writing

An undesirable and poorly constructed thesis share the following common errors, mistakes, or logical flaws.

ABSTRACT

A common mistake novice writers make in the abstract is providing a simple summary of the research/thesis. A novice writer in academic English also often makes the mistake of utilizing patch−writing to complete an abstract, meaning pieces from the main thesis text are patched together to form an abstract. As mentioned earlier, your abstract is your book cover. Will you copy and paste some words and sentences from your book to create the book cover and title? Will people feel intrigued to pick up and buy that book? No. The abstract is where a writer's skillfulness and complete understanding of the research and content of the thesis come together. It should be as original as any other writing you did.

INTRODUCTION

An undesirable introduction does not explicitly state the problem. There are no proper logical explanations that provide rationales for the problem or the research being conducted. Furthermore, if there is no explicit statement of the research purpose and/or research questions, the readers are instantly lost and drawn away to further engage with your thesis or your research. Without the research question(s) or hypotheses established, it is difficult to know what the researcher has intended to investigate.

LITERATURE REVIEW

Typically, a novice writer fails to provide a well−synthesized literature review. This means the literature review reads like a list of summaries of previous research rather than offering a central theme or message from the review literature. Furthermore, this central theme or message from previous literature makes insufficient connections between the variables and the theoretical framework. A failure to explain why the theoretical or conceptual framework is suitable for the purpose of the research gives little reason for the readers to continue reading your thesis. Also, if the gap in pre−existing literature is not addressed, your thesis will lack the reasoning to conduct your research.

METHODOLOGY/RESEARCH DESIGN

A poorly written methodology section does not specify the rationale for selecting the specific design and methodology. This results in a misalignment between the research design, methodology, and research procedures. Evidently, the misalignment commonly occurs between the research design and the theoretical or conceptual framework. Keep in mind that the research purpose and questions, research design, methodology, and theoretical/conceptual framework are seamlessly interrelated and interconnected.

FINDINGS/RESULTS

Typically, a novice writer struggles to present the research findings/results in an organized manner. In this case, the reader cannot follow the findings/results logically. Another common mistake is a failure to select and present the right data. A novice researcher and writer may feel the obligation to report absolutely everything generated from the data analysis instead of sorting the absolutely essential information. Although all the data collected are valuable, it is important to prioritize and select the data and present the findings that contribute to building your central message aligned with your research questions/hypotheses. Furthermore, ensure that your findings/results are presented in a manner in which the core results are highlighted to shed light on the research topic rather than highlighting the researcher's data analysis process in its raw form.

DISCUSSION/CONCLUSION

The discussion/conclusion section is the biggest challenge to a novice writer and researcher. A common error that occurs by novice researchers and writers is providing a simple summary of the research findings/results in the discussion section instead of articulating how the results from previous research align or diverge from the current study. The research also may fail to answer the essential "so what?" question, meaning the originality of the research is challenging to discern, with little or no evidence for future directions and implications.

▶ Chart the central themes of pre−existing research addressing similar problems you intend to address. How can your research stand out from the existing body of literature?

▶ What are the qualities you need to work on in order to construct a research writing piece or thesis that is strong and well−organized?

Planning and Preparation Stages

 Opening Questions

- What are your ideas and plans for your research project?
- What specific steps and tasks can you outline for a research project from start to finish?
- How prepared do you feel to initiate and start your research and writing?

 In this chapter, you will···

- Apply the basic structure of an introduction in your research planning.
- Formulate purposes for your research and scholarly identities.

When entering the planning phase for your research and thesis, it is imperative to know and understand the typical stages involved in the entire thesis writing process. Thesis writing, like any other research project, is a multi−year process. Knowing not only your destination but also the stops and routes leading to your destination is critical in the long journey of thesis writing. This understanding provides guidance on organizing and formulating your research during the preparatory phase.

Steps for Research and Thesis Writing

What are the recommended research steps for conducting thesis research and writing? While there is not one definitive rule of a singular approach to completing thesis research and writing, there are commonly adopted steps that will enhance the efficiency and rigor of your research and writing processes. These recommended research steps play a vital role in crafting academic papers and completing a high−quality thesis. Bear in mind that the research and thesis writing process is not a straight−forward journey but rather complex and dynamic in nature. This means, some of these steps outlined below may sound repetitive or redundant at times. The nature of this process is interwoven, complicated, and sometimes cyclical.

Step 1. Identify educational or societal issues aligning with your research interest, field, and topic.

Step 2. Formulate a previse **problem statement** and articulate the purpose of your study, seeking guidance from your faculty advisor and/or committee members.

Step 3. Review prior studies related to the research topic/keywords and delve into a specialized area.

Step 4. Define your research question(s) or hypotheses and draft the **introduction** of your thesis.

Step 5. Explore and comprehend the theory applicable to the research subject.

Step 6. Summarize previous studies on the subject and research topic/issue. Refine the **introduction** and **literature review** sections accordingly, seeking feedback from your faculty advisor or committee chair as much as possible.

Step 7. Identify an appropriate research methodology to address the research question(s) or hypotheses. Draft the **methodology/research design** section while consulting with our faculty advisor or committee chair.

Step 8. Gather documents necessary for the IRB application and review (see Chapter 5 for details).

Step 9. Once approved by IRB, collect and analyze data using the proposed research methodology. Refine the **methodology/research design** section. Seek guidance from your faculty advisor or committee chair as needed.

Step 10. During and after the data analysis process, search and outline a few approaches to present and articulate the **findings/results** effectively.

Step 11. Draft the **discussion/conclusion** section, consulting with your faculty advisor or committee chair.

Step 12. Implement necessary revisions and maintain ongoing communication with your faculty advisor or committee chair.

We strongly advise adhering to the steps above as you undertake the task of research and thesis writing. It is especially crucial to approach the process by taking the necessary preparatory measures prior to the data collection stage. It is a common mistake novice researchers and writers make to collect data first or select the population or group they prefer to collect data from before conducting an in−depth literature review (see Chapter 10 for details) or laying a strong foundation with a problem statement and research purpose. Furthermore, it is vital to explore prior research documented and published in English, as many international researchers choose English−language channels to disseminate their most impactful work. Likewise, it is crucial for beginning international scholars to enhance their proficiency in academic English writing to have a more significant impact on their future research within the academic field.

Organization of an Introduction

The introduction section provides an overview of the entire research and thesis. An

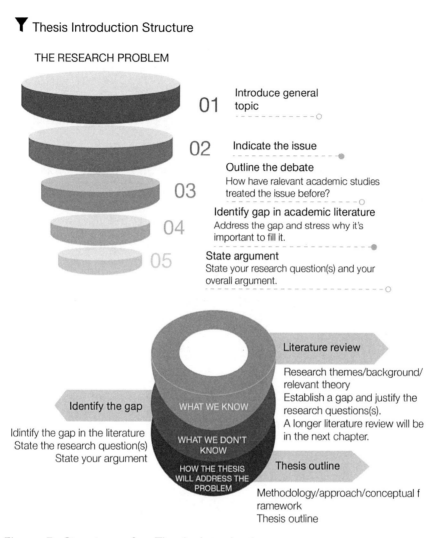

▼ Thesis Introduction Structure

THE RESEARCH PROBLEM

01 Introduce general topic

02 Indicate the issue

Outline the debate
How have ralevant academic studies treated the issue before?

03

Identify gap in academic literature
Address the gap and stress why it's important to fill it.

04

State argument
State your research question(s) and your overall argument.

05

Identify the gap
Idintify the gap in the literature
State the research question(s)
State your argument

WHAT WE KNOW

WHAT WE DON'T KNOW

HOW THE THESIS WILL ADDRESS THE PROBLEM

Literature review
Research themes/background/ relevant theory
Establish a gap and justify the research questions(s).
A longer literature review will be in the next chapter.

Thesis outline
Methodology/approach/conceptual f ramework
Thesis outline

Figure 5. Structure of a Thesis Introduction

introduction is a rather challenging section to write for novice writers; this is because the introduction requires summarizing skills, conciseness, and in−depth knowledge of the field and the research presented. Figure 5 depicts the "funnel" structure in the introduction of a thesis or research writing. Similar to a funnel's broad opening that sifts content through, your introduction follows a logical progression. By beginning to address the general educational landscape, you filter out other issues and concentrate on a specific problem on which your research intends to focus. Subsequently, you outline previously researched areas to fill the gaps in existing research, substantiating the rationale for your study.

Preparation Stage: Thinking about the Why, What, and How

As you embark on the preparatory stage of your research and thesis writing, thinking about the why, what, and how can be central to guiding your research and writing process. Like we said earlier, a thesis writing and research project can easily take a few years to complete. If you lose direction to answer the why, what, and how questions, you can easily lose your motivation and inspiration to continue on, especially at difficult moments. Think about the following questions, and every now and then, come back to them to see if your answers have changed or if you need to remind yourself why you started this journey.

THINKING ABOUT THE "WHY"

Why am I writing and researching this?. There are not enough ways to emphasize the importance of identifying and elucidating the educational problem or issue that will be the focus of your research. If your approach to thesis writing and research is solely focused on obtaining a degree and graduating, it will inevitably compromise the quality of your work. Furthermore, you will find yourself sailing without a destination and a reason to weather through the challenges you encounter. Pursuing a graduate degree with a thesis and research project implies the expectation of developing profound insights, critical thinking skills, and innovative approaches to problem–solving. Your motivation should be driven by a grand societal issue and larger purpose with the intent to address a specific problem in your field. Why did you decide to pursue a graduate degree in the first place? As an emerging scholar, which problem do you aim to solve, and why are you passionate about it? Answering these questions will help you maintain your focus as you work towards completing your thesis writing and research.

Why is engaging in scholarly communications in English important?. As an emerging scholar, you should engage in scholarly communications and discussions in English, including literature review and academic writing in English. Your proficiency in comprehending and producing scholarly texts in English contributes to developing skills to publish research articles in international journals and present at global academic conferences. Proficiency in reading and writing research in English facilitates your integration into the broader global research community. Rather than perceiving this as a mere requirement for successfully defending your thesis and obtaining a degree, consider it as an opportunity for ongoing life skills development as a global citizen and scholar. Acquiring academic communication skills in English is a fundamental capability for evolving into a global researcher and scholar. Whether you choose to actively participate in your local community or involve yourself in professional groups in your home country, your status as a global citizen remains unchanged. English, as an international lingua franca, retains its significance, evidenced by its recognition as the sole working language for the Association of South East Asian Nations (ASEAN). In our global society with constant transnational exchange and mobility, enhancing your English proficiency for academic communication brings numerous advantages.

THINKING ABOUT THE "WHAT"

What will be the educational impact after conducting this research?. Initially, ponder the educational problem(s) or issue(s) you aim to address or solve. Subsequently, assess the potential educational ramifications that may arise from undertaking your research. The impact within the educational field encompasses the development or alteration of academic/education programs, advancing the discussion in the field, improving student outcomes, or contributing to educators' professional development. On a micro level, your research can provide opportunities to enhance, amend, or formulate courses/curricula applicable to K−12 or postsecondary education settings. On a macro level, your research may have the potential to question or alter established ideologies, perceptions, or approaches in the field of education. Regardless of whether the impact is substantial or modest, it is essential to consider the ripple effects your research may generate.

What are the central and pivotal discussions surrounding the issue?. Maintaining knowledge of current scholarly trends, discussions, and up−to−date information makes the justification of the "why" and "what impact" easier. As highlighted earlier, this is another reason why engaging in scholarly communications in English is crucial. Without knowing what research has been done and to which direction the scholarly interest is shifting, your research can be easily perceived as a repetition of previous research and a statement of the obvious facts that have been discovered. The advancement of technology has enabled the process of knowledge exchange to be more seamless and faster than ever. This means every year and every month, you need to check and read new scholarly articles related to your research topic to maintain the relevance of your research. This also allows you to construct a more logical argument about the issue or problem at hand.

THINKING ABOUT THE "HOW"

How do I conduct meaningful research that will make an educational impact?. As you gear up for your thesis writing and research, you should check if your thesis is making a meaningful contribution and impact to your field. For emerging scholars and novice academic writers, it is not the easiest task to assess whether you are making a significant contribution or not. If your research aligns with any of the following conditions, your research might be heading in the right direction.

- The research topic displays originality, delving into new keywords that have not been adequately examined.
- The research context is distinctive, focusing on an environment where existing research has not been thoroughly explored.
- The study subjects are unique, with previous research failing to include this particular group as participants.
- The research demonstrates proficiency and/or innovation in applying research methodology or approach.

How should I establish my identity as a researcher and scholar?. As an emerging researcher, it might be difficult to establish your identity as a legitimate researcher and scholar at first. However, Rome was not built in a day, and neither is your identity and status. The foundation of constructing and establishing a scholarly identity is to gain a comprehensive understanding of your research and the field. This entails acquiring proficiency in both quantitative and qualitative research methods regardless of what you are specializing in and how you plan to conduct your thesis research. Individuals primarily engaged in quantitative research should familiarize themselves with papers utilizing qualitative research methodology, while those predominantly involved in qualitative research should read and comprehend the interpretation of quantitative research methodology and findings. A well−rounded knowledge of all research methods adds to your level of confidence and your ability to navigate a broader domain of research. Keep in mind that you are fostering a growth mindset, embodying a researcher who is consistently engaged and eager to learn, inquiry, and explore throughout your career and lifetime.

▸ Start outlining the introduction of your academic writing by implementing the funnel structure. What is the most difficult part to write down and why?

Introduce general topic — What is the general topic you plan to address? --

Indicate the issue — What is the problem/issue? --

Outline the debate — What does previous research say about this? ------------------------------

Identify the gap — What remains unaddressed or unsolved? -----------------------------

State argument — What is your argument/purpose? ---

▸Think about your what, why, and how. Remember, come back to these questions and your answers later.

Why am I writing and researching this?	
Why is engaging in scholarly communications in English important?	
What will be the educational impact after conducting this research?	
What are the central and pivotal discussions surrounding the issue?	
How do I conduct meaningful research that will make an educational impact?	
How should I establish my identity as a researcher and scholar?	

08

Establishing the Problem
: Problem-solving Research Method

 Opening Questions

- What does it mean to establish a problem or problematize?
- How can a problem−solving stance and approach apply to your research?
- What challenges do you anticipate in the problem−solving research method?

 In this chapter, you will⋯

- Articulate the steps and procedures of applying a problem−solving research method.
- Formulate statements to establish a problem for your research.

As you embark on the process of thesis writing and research, a foundational step involves going beyond simple identification of a problem; this means meticulously establishing the problem you intend to address. Approach this important stage with a proactive problem−solving stance. What does a problem−solving stance entail? This involves delving into the intricacies of the issue, understanding its nuances, and discerning the underlying challenges.

What is a Problem-solving Approach?

To exemplify this problem−solving research approach, let's consider a scenario where the identified problem pertains to educational disparities in a specific region. A common error novice scholars and writers make in this stage is simply describing or stating the problem, such as the outcomes in students' English writing achievements in Korean high schools being below the standard level of achievements. This may look like a problem at a glance, but in actuality, it is a mere description of a problem or a statement of a fact. The next step, problematizing the problem through a problem−solving stance, needs to take place. Instead of merely acknowledging the existence of the problem, a problem−solving stance would involve an in−depth exploration of its root causes, examining the contributing factors, and critically assessing potential solutions. By going beyond the surface level, a problem−solving research approach aims to develop comprehensive insights that will inform meaningful interventions or solutions.

Research Example 1

A comparative investigation into multicultural and multilingual teacher education in two countries: The United States and South Korea

- *Identifying the problem*: In comparison to the multicultural and multilingual teacher education programs in the United States, the educational system in South Korea lacks perspectives on teacher education.

- *Problem−solving approach*: Is it viable to develop a model for multicultural and multilingual teacher education in South Korean higher education by implementing a model from the U.S. teacher education program?

- *Reviewing research*: Examining existing research in the following areas may be beneficial. (a) Current teacher education in the United States utilizes translanguaging pedagogy as a theoretical foundation for approaching multicultural and multilingual teacher education. And (b) Prior studies employed translanguaging pedagogy in teacher education, preferably in Asian teacher education contexts.

- *Implementing solution*: As you consider a few viable solutions, answering these questions might be helpful. Can a straightforward comparative analysis between the two countries resolve the identified problem? Is it practical to propose a model for multicultural and multilingual teacher education considering the context in South Korea?

As outlined in Research Example 1, employing a problem−solving approach enabled the researcher to undertake the study with a discerning outlook. As an emerging scholar growing up and being exposed to the active global knowledge exchange and market, you have a unique advantage in conducting comparative research. You may have experiences, knowledge, or insights to contemplate two distinct educational systems. The following problem statement can be formulated, deriving from a problem−solving approach:

The deficiency of a multicultural and multilingual perspective in South Korea's teacher education program arises from the absence of a systematically designed teacher education curriculum tailored to multicultural and multilingual students' needs.

Even when pondering a rather practical research question and problem in Research Example 2, a problem−solving approach can be beneficial.

- *Identifying the problem*: The conventional face-to-face setting for pre-service teachers' micro-teaching task encountered a challenge in the context of the COVID-19 emergency remote learning environment.

- *Problem-solving approach*: An introduction of an online teaching method within education courses focusing on the online micro-teaching experience for pre-service teachers.

- *Reviewing research*: Previous literature has measured face-to-face micro-teaching with various variables, but the application of these measurements to online teacher education courses remains limited and rather inconclusive. However, research on online and blended learning has evolved since the 1990s, emphasizing a community of inquiry framework.

- *Reflective stage*: It is beneficial to consider a few reflective questions upon review of existing research as you formulate solutions. Is it still appropriate to apply existing variables and measurements from face-to-face micro-teaching research? Can the study incorporate and extend the community of inquiry framework into an online micro-teaching context?

- *Implementing solution*: A few solutions could be generated as your research seeks to design a practical program or curriculum. Can the incorporation of gamification of learning into online micro-teaching, integrated with the concepts of teaching and social presence in the community of inquiry framework, offer fresh insights for enhancing the online teacher education program?

Research example 2 introduced an unforeseen factor, notably the COVID-10 emergency remote learning context. Unlike conventional online degree programs, both pre-service teachers and teacher educators in this scenario lack proficiency in digital literacies and competence in online teaching methods. Given these challenges, adopting a problem-solving approach can be crucial to offering solutions. A problem—solving stance allowed the researcher to broaden the search by looking into other areas of research in order to find viable solutions. In this example, the following problem statement could be formulated:

The efficacy of online micro—teaching activities for pre—service teachers in South Korea during the COVID—19 pandemic is compromised due to the absence of models for transitioning an in—person teacher education program to a remote curriculum.

As illustrated in these two examples, a problem—solving stance and approach entails investigating cause, effect, and closely related subjects. By adopting a problem—solving stance, it was possible to interrogate the problem beyond a mere description, leading to envisioning a few possible solutions.

The Cyclical Steps of a Problem-solving Research Method

In essence, adopting a problem—solving stance in research and thesis writing requires a commitment to not only recognizing the problem but actively engaging with the problem at hand. This means asking probing questions, seeking a thorough understanding of the context, and envisioning viable solutions. This approach, as a research method, strengthens the foundation of your research and, more importantly, contributes to the advancement of knowledge within your field of study.

Figure 6 provides a visual representation of the iterative stages involved in employing a problem—solving research method. This approach is not a straightforward, linear process but rather operates as a cyclical sequence. The steps involved in this cyclical problem—solving approach are elaborated below:

DEFINE THE PROBLEM

In this initial step, you need to identify and articulate the issue you plan to address. This involves a thorough understanding of the scope, context, and factors relating to the problem. Furthermore, a comprehensive exploration of the problem, ensuring clarity as you formulate the problem is necessary. You should specify the boundary

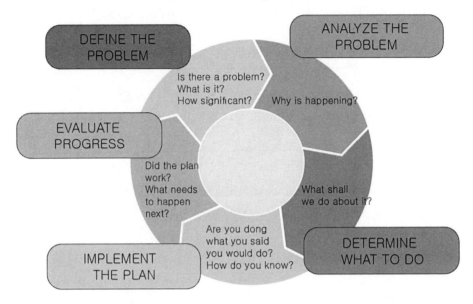

Figure 6. The Cycle of a Problem-solving Research Method

of the problem and consider various perspectives (i.e., various philosophies, approaches, contexts, factors, etc.) as you do so.

ANALYZE THE PROBLEM

The analysis phase involves a detailed examination of the problem you identified. You should evaluate the cause, implication, and potential impact of the problem in a broader context. Try to employ different analytical tools, resources, and methodologies to uncover hidden aspects of the problem. As illustrated in Research Example 2, sometimes solutions exist in places remotely or closely related to your research focus. This means analyzing the problem from all angles, and perspectives may lead you to innovative approaches to solving the problem.

DECIDE HOW AND WHAT TO DO

Following a thorough analysis, the next step is to determine the most effective approach to addressing the problem. This involves an in-depth understanding and specific identification of the problem. The broader the problem is, the more difficult it will be to approach solving it. Utilizing your comprehensive knowledge concerning the stated problem, you should weigh the pros and cons, anticipate potential challenges, and consider the applicability of your solutions.

IMPLEMENT THE PLAN IN THE FIELD

With a well−defined problem and solution in place, you should proceed to implement the solution. This phase is two−fold. First, in the planning stage of establishing the problem for your research, this means articulating the solution, which will be your research purpose, research question(s), hypotheses, or intervention(s). Second, in a larger context, this applies to your research process, in which you will conduct your research based on the problems and plans you have established. At this juncture, we focus on emphasizing the former than the latter. The latter will become more relevant as we discuss wrapping up your research and thesis in Chapter 12.

EVALUATE THE PROGRESS

The evaluation stage assesses the outcomes and progress resulting from the implemented plan. You will gauge the effectiveness, realistic implication, practical application, and impact of the implementation plan. As mentioned above, this is applicable to the problem establishment stage as well as concluding your entire research project. Considering the process of establishing a problem this entails outlining the appropriate research measurements and evaluating their applicability. The cyclical nature of the problem−solving research method allows for iteration. If the evaluation reveals shortcomings, limited impact, or challenges to practical implementation, you should revisit earlier stages, particularly returning to the problem definition phase.

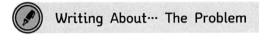

Writing About··· The Problem

Knowing "what" to write in theory is one problem; knowing "how" to write in practice is another problem. In the "Writing About" section, we offer a small inventory of possible language and writing structures you can implement in your writing practices. A few language functions you want to be familiar with when it comes to problem statement and establishment are: establishing a research territory, identifying the research/knowledge gap, and stating your research purpose.

ESTABLISHING A RESEARCH TERRITORY

Establishing a research territory refers to setting the context, defining the scope, and identifying existing knowledge or debates within a particular subject area. The following are some possible language inventory items:

- **Through** broadening literacy frameworks, **the** literacy **field increasingly recognizes** the social and political dynamics of texts and their production.
  - Bacon, C. K. (2017). Multilanguage, multipurpose: A literature review, synthesis, and framework for critical literacies in English language teaching. Journal of Literacy Research. 49(3). 424−453.

- **Studies have repeatedly shown that** English language learners (ELLs) in elementary and secondary schools are frustrated because the school system is failing to support them in achieving their goals of acquiring English and obtaining postsecondary education (Menken, 2008; Olsen, 1997; Suarez−Orozco, Suarez−Orozco, & Todorova, 2008; Valdés, 2001).
  - Daniel, S. M. (2014). Learning to educate English language learners in pre−service elementary practicums. *Teacher Education Quarterly, Spring 2014*, 5−28.

- **There is currently an upsurge of interest in all matters** emotional and affective **in** education. **First popularised by** Daniel Goleman (1995; Hartley, 2003), emotional intelligence **is set to become a** mainstream curricular concern for teachers at all levels, including pre−service teacher education (Hawkey, 2006).

- • Hawkey, K. (2006). Emotional intelligence and mentoring in pre−service teacher education: A literature review. *Mentoring & Tutoring.* 14(2), 137−147.

- **Much recent literature on** teacher education **highlights the importance of** identity in teacher development.

  - • Beauchamp, C. & Thomas, L. (2009). Understanding teacher identity: an overview of issues in the literature and implications for teacher education. *Cambridge Journal of Education*, 39(2), 175−189.

IDENTIFYING THE RESEARCH/KNOWLEDGE GAP

Identifying research or knowledge gap involves pinpointing areas within the established research territory where existing research is limited, incomplete, or lacks sufficient exploration. This is essential for your research and thesis writing as it justifies the need for the study by demonstrating that there is a specific question, issue, or aspect that has not been adequately addressed in the existing literature.

- **These studies have made a persuasive case for the** multidimensional role of emotions in teachers' professional development and in their day−to−day teaching lives, **though they have not necessarily suggested** interventional responses to acknowledge, mitigate, or improve teachers' emotional stances systematically. **The question persists:** How does a language teacher educator make sense of the pervasive emotional content present in novice teacher reflection journals as they react to their initial teaching experiences in the language classroom?

  - • Golombek, P. & Doran, M. (2014). Unifying cognition, emotion, and activity in language teacher professional development. Teaching and Teacher Education, 39(2014), 102−111.

- **More** teacher education **work is needed to lay the foundation for** and approximate the teaching of linguistically diverse students.

- Athanases, S. & Wong, J. W. (2018). Learning from analyzing linguistically diverse students' work: A contribution of preservice teacher inquiry. *The Educational Forum*, 82(2), 191−207

- **Attention is paid to** core practices across subjects and grade levels, including, for example, leading a discussion or eliciting student thinking (Ball & Forzani, 2009 ; Dotger, 2015 ; Kavanagh & Rainey, 2017). **However,** developing TE pedagogies for core practices in work with linguistically diverse learners **has been less fully realized.**
  - Athanases, S. Z. & Wong, J. W. (2018). Learning from analyzing linguistically diverse students' work: A contribution of preservice teacher inquiry. *The Educational forum*, 82(2), 191−207.

- **Although extensive research has been carried out on the** teacher knowledge base **in general** (Bransford, Brown, & Cocking, 1999; Grossman, 1990; Grossman, Wilson, & Shulman, 1989; Guerrero, 2005; Nespor, 1987; Pajares, 1992; Shulman, 1987) **and** ESL teacher cognition (Franco−Fuenmayor, Padrón, & Waxman, 2015; Freeman & Johnson, 1998; Gatbonton, 2008; Johnston & Goettsch, 2006; Kanno & Stuart, 2011; Kubanyiova & Feryok, 2015; Liu, 2013; Wright, 2010), **there has been no detailed investigations of** what mainstream teachers already know and what they need to learn to support ELLs in their classrooms.
  - Hilliker, S. & Laletina, A. (2018). What do mainstream teachers think, know, and think they know about English language learners? *NYS TESOL Journal*, 5(1), 30−50.

- **Such efforts, though important, fail to address** more diverse education classes and PSTs of color who often call for more attention to their experiences, needs, and preparedness to teach culturally and linguistically diverse students and to explore nuanced differences, multiple intersectionalities, and hybrid identities.

- Athanases, S. Z., Banes, L. C., & Wong , J. W. (2015). Diverse language profiles: Leveraging resources of potential bilingual teachers of color. *Bilingual Research Journal, 38*(1), 65−87.

STATING YOUR RESEARCH PURPOSE

Stating the research purpose entails clearly and concisely articulating the primary objective or goal of the research study. This guides your readers through the study's intent and provides a focused direction for your research.

- **In this paper, we propose** an alternative approach to rubrics−based classroom assessment.
  - Fang, Z., & Wang, Z. (2011). Beyond rubrics: Using functional language analysis to evaluate student writing. *Australian Journal of Language & Literacy,* 34(2), 147−165.

- **This article presents** a teacher preparation model—a language−based approach to content instruction (LACI)— developed over the past 10 years of research in content area classrooms with English language learners (ELLs) and based on recent scholarship on the language demands of schooling
  - de Oliveira, L. C. (2016). A language−based approach to content instruction (LACI) for English language learners: Examples from two elementary teachers. *International Multilingual Research Journal.* 10(3), 217−231.

- **The purpose of this paper is to provide an overview of the issues related to** teacher identity **stemming from recent literature and to suggest the implications for** effective teacher education embedded in the discussion of these issues.
  - Beauchamp, C. & Thomas, L. (2009). Understanding teacher identity: an overview of issues in the literature and implications for teacher education. *Cambridge Journal of Education, 39*(2), 175−189.

- **In the present study, we focus on** a core practice of reviewing and carefully assessing student work, with attention to viewing that work as language and meaning in process.

  - Athanases, S. & Wong, J. W. (2018). Learning from analyzing linguistically diverse students' work: A contribution of preservice teacher inquiry. *The Educational Forum, 82*(2), 191 – 207

- **We aim to add to this body of literature concerning** the education and experiences of prospective Latino/a teachers **and to see** how their concerns, strengths, hopes, and struggles are negotiated in their program of teacher education, whom they see themselves teaching, and how they imagine working with children and youth.

  - Gomez , M. L. , Rodriguez , T. L. , & Agosto , V. (2008). Life histories of Latino/a teacher candidates. *Teachers College Record, 110*(8), 1639-1676.

▶ Try applying the problem−solving research method as an outlining tool. What is the most challenging step(s) in the cycle of a problem−solving research method?

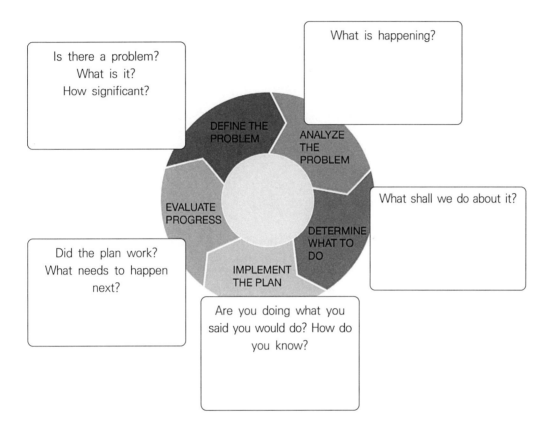

▶ Start writing about the problem by establishing a research territory, identifying the research/knowledge gap, and stating your research purpose. Where do you get stuck formulating statements, and why do you think that is?

Establishing a Theoretical Foundation

 Opening Questions

- What is your understanding of a theoretical foundation? Why do you think a strong theoretical foundation is important?
- How would you begin the process of establishing a theoretical foundation for your research?

 In this chapter, you will…

- Distinguish approaches to establish a strong theoretical foundation.
- Select an approach to build a theoretical foundation for your research.

What does it mean to establish a theoretical foundation, and why is it important to establish a strong theoretical framework? Establishing a robust theoretical framework is essential for solidifying the arguments you intend to convey in your research and providing a structured method to navigate your research purpose and goals. A well–researched theoretical foundation not only lends credibility to your research but also facilitates a systematic approach to data collection and analysis.

Integrating Theory into Your Research

We recommend three primary avenues through which you can effectively integrate theory into your research and thesis writing:

Draw from established work: One strategy involves seeking out and incorporating a theoretical framework from a recognized scholar in the field. Established theoretical frameworks often provide fundamental tenets and concepts, along with associated methodologies for data collection and analysis. This approach anchors your research in well–established principles, enhancing the reliability and coherence of your study.

Construct a conceptual framework: Another viable approach is to construct a conceptual framework by integrating or modifying existing theories. Researchers often meld two or three theories or frameworks to align with their specific research purpose, context, or chosen methodology. This approach allows some flexibility and customization to tailor your theoretical foundation to the unique demands of your research. It also opens up a great opportunity to draw on theories and concepts from other fields and subject areas, making it possible to propose innovative approaches to address the problem or issue outlined in your study.

Grounded theory for unexplored territories: In cases where the research delves into uncharted territories, a grounded theory approach becomes an option. Grounded theory involves a nuanced and time–intensive process where theories are formed and established by grounding your research in the data. This can be particularly challenging for novice researchers. We advise novice researchers to defer this approach until sufficient expertise is acquired, and therefore, we will not focus on the grounded theory approach in this book.

By establishing a strong theoretical foundation, you not only demonstrate your scholarly rigor but also pave the way for a more nuanced and insightful exploration of your research questions. The theoretical framework acts as a guide, shaping the direction of your study and providing a solid foundation for the interpretation of your findings/results.

Drawing from Established Work

A great approach to initiating your research and establishing a theoretical foundation is drawing from seminal work. Particularly for novice and emerging scholars, we advise surveying seminal work before deciding which approach you would like to take with your research. Generally, quantitative research employs a theoretical framework to assess existing theories, while qualitative research aims to construct or enhance theories. However, this is not a hard−and−fast rule—there are numerous exceptions. When adopting well−established theoretical approaches, it is crucial to exercise caution to ensure the originality of your research rather than duplicating prior studies.

Given the extensive scholarly exploration of social and educational phenomena in the field of educational research, crafting original research can pose a significant challenge to emerging scholars. By conducting a thorough survey and review of existing theories and empirical research, you will be able to add more originality to your research that can change or contribute to the discussions in your field.

Illustrated in Figure 7 is the cycle of theory, research, and practice. This is essential for researchers to be cognizant of as they establish the theoretical foundation of their research. Your research rooted in theory contributes to the transformation of real−life practices, subsequently influencing theory and research once again. It is imperative to consider how your theory−based research can be practically applied in the educational field to address academic and societal issues. This practical

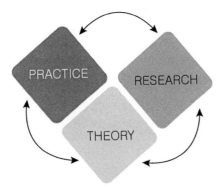

Figure 7. Cycle of Theory, Research, and Practice

application represents the educational or scholarly value of your research as you strategize and conceptualize your research and thesis.

Constructing a Conceptual Framework

A conceptual framework can play a critical role in empirical research. Conceptual frameworks allow researchers to put intentional effort into connecting diverse perspectives and aspects. Furthermore, developing a conceptual framework by adjusting or merging two or more theories can suggest new and novel perspectives. Because of these reasons, a conceptual framework is understood to be a great way to demonstrate how the researchers rigorously and appropriately answered the research questions.

Researchers frequently acknowledge the limitations of employing one theoretical perspective and seek additional theories, sometimes from different fields. This helps to address specific shortcomings of a single theoretical framework. For instance, Kim (2021) constructed a conceptual framework drawing from a theory called Dialogical Selves and research insights from empirical research on language teacher identities in order to answer the following research questions: (a) How do elementary teacher candidates construct professional identities in the context of teaching English language learners (ELLs)? And (b) What language−related experiences shape teacher candidates' growing professional identities as teachers of ELLs? Due to the limited empirical research on language teacher identities of mainstream elementary teacher candidates, the author drew on a theoretical framework to help examine general teacher and teacher candidates' professional identities. In addition, the author added important findings from the body of research on language teacher identities in order to add analytical tools for examining language−related experiences (see Figure 8).

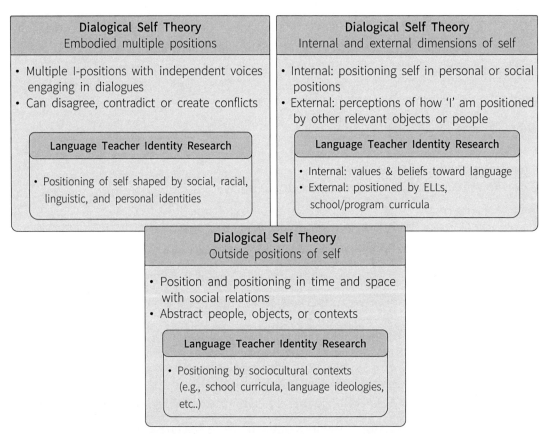

Figure 8. Sample Conceptual Framework: Research and Theoretical Strands of Dialogical Teacher Professional Identities (Kim, 2021)

This particular approach, constructing conceptual frameworks, offers a distinct advantage in the discussion section as you are reinterpreting the data and results. Not only has the research integrated multiple theoretical concepts to broaden methodological possibilities, but it also implemented a conceptual framework to reshape and potentially propose a new emerging theory informed by the data collected from the research study. This approach easily adds originality to the researcher's work, which will inform practice and theories again.

 Writing About⋯ The Problem

In this "Writing About" section, we offer an inventory of language to write about the theoretical foundation. A few language functions helpful for establishing a theoretical foundation are: defining concepts/terms/objects and classifying and categorizing.

DEFINING CONCEPTS/TERMS/OBJECTS

Defining occurs more often in academic writing than what you might anticipate. Due to its rather straightforward purpose (defining), the statements written by novice writers often remain stagnant, repetitive, and sometimes boring. The following are some other options to define concepts, terms, or objects:

- Identity **can be conceptualized as** "stories to live by" (Clandinin, Downey, & Huber, 2009, p. 141) **or as** "those narratives about individuals that are reifying, endorsable and significant" (Sfard & Prusak, 2005, p.16).
  - Dinham, J., Chalk, B., Beltman, S., Glass, C., & Nguyen, B. (2017). Pathways to resilience: how drawings reveal pre−service teachers' core narratives underpinning their future teacher−selves. *Asia−Pacific Journal of Teacher Education*, 45(2), 126−144.

- **The concept of** the index has particular value for construing the role of emotions as one of signaling, or pointing to, areas of nascent cognitive development in the teacher learner. **Simply put**, when a teacher expresses an emotion, the message of that underlying response is an indexical 'look here, pay attention to this' relative to some area of cognitive understanding.
  - Golombek, P. & Doran, M. (2014). Unifying cognition, emotion, and activity in language teacher professional development. *Teaching and Teacher Education, 39* (2014), 102−111.

- English language learners (ELLs)—that is, students who speak a first language other than English—now account for nearly 10% of the U.S. public school student population (Kena et al., 2016).

  - Lucas, T., Strom, K., Bratkovich, M., & Wnuk, J. (2018). Inservice preparation for mainstream teachers of English language learners: A review of the empirical literature. The Educational Forum, 82(2), 156−173.

- My use of the term academic knowledge includes both the knowledge acquired in arts and science and education courses.

  - Zeichner, K. (2010). Rethinking the connections between campus courses and field experiences in college- and university-based teacher education. *Journal of Teacher Education, 61*(1-2), 89-99.

- Cochran−Smith and Lytle (1993) define teacher research as "systematic, intentional inquiry by teachers" (p. 5)

  - Dana, N. F., Yendol−Hoppey, D., & Snow−Gerono (2006). Deconstructing inquiry in the professional development school: Exploring the domains and contents of teachers' questions. Action in Teacher Education, 27(4), 59−71.

COMPARING & CONTRASTING

Comparing and contrasting is a useful strategy and function in any situation. From establishing problem to concluding your research, you can make good use of comparing and contrasting to make meaningful statements. The following inventory of language can help you begin comparing and contrasting:

- It should be stated that there are epistemological differences between translanguaging and code−switching even though instances of the latter may be part of the former. Unlike code−switching, which refers to the use of two or more separate languages and the shifting of one code to another (Hornberger & Link, 2012), translanguaging does not recognise boundaries between languages, but focuses on what the speakers do with their language repertoires. From these repertoires, the speakers 'select language features and soft assemble their language practices in ways that fit their communicative needs' (García, 2011: 7). Furthermore, code−switching often carries language−centred connotations of language interference, transfer or borrowing of codes (see also Makalela, 2013) **while** translanguaging shifts lens from cross−linguistic influence to how multilinguals intermingle linguistic features (Hornberger & Link, 2012: 263).

- Makalela, L. (2015). Translanguaging as a vehicle for epistemic access: Cases for reading comprehension and multilingual interactions. *Per Linguam: a Journal of Language Learning= Per Linguam: Tydskrif vir Taalaanleer, 31*(1), 15−29.

- The main disputes within this framework arise over whether state interests will be served by engaging in particular interventions. **By contrast,** studies informed by alternative mapping and nontechnical issues: utopianism, cosmopolitanism, constructivism, and postmodernism, have been relatively few and far between, overshadowed by policy−driven concerns.

  - Pugh, M. (2004). Peacekeeping and critical theory. *International peacekeeping, 11*(1), 39−58.

- Across educational attainment levels, there appears to be no relationship between educational attainment and the belief that war is sometimes or always justified in Jordan and Pakistan. **In contrast,** it appears as if educational attainment is associated with believing that war is sometimes or always justified in Lebanon and Turkey.

  - Shafiq, M. N. & Ross, K. (2010). Educational attainment and attitudes towards war in Muslim countries contemplating war: The cases of Jordan, Lebanon, Pakistan, and Turkey. Journal of Development Studies, 46(8), 1424−1441.

- While the defining characteristic of neo−liberalism is largely based on the central tenets of classical liberalism, in particular classic economic liberalism, **there are crucial differences between** classical liberalism and neo−

liberalism. **These differences** are absolutely essential in understanding the politics of education and the transformations education is currently undergoing. Mark Olssen (1996) **clearly details these differences** in the following passage.

- Apple, M. (2001). Comparing neo−liberal projects and inequality in education. Comparative Education, 37(4), 409−423.

- Finland was the **top overall performer among** OECD countries in 2000 and 2003 PISA studies, and **the only** country that was able to improve performance.
  - Sahlberg, P. (2011). PISA in Finland: An education miracle or an obstacle to change?. *CEPS Journal: Center for Educational Policy Studies Journal, 1*(3), 119.

- More than half of Finnish students reached level 4 or higher in reading literacy, **in comparison to** the United States, where only approximately one quarter of all students were able to do the same.
  - Sahlberg, P. (2011). PISA in Finland: An education miracle or an obstacle to change?. *CEPS Journal: Center for Educational Policy Studies Journal, 1*(3), 119.

- The variation in HDI explains 54% of the between−country variation in civic knowledge, showing that national averages of civic knowledge are related to factors reflecting the general development and wellbeing of a country. **This finding is similar to those from** other international studies of educational outcomes; however, it does not necessarily mean that there is a causal relationship between civic knowledge and the overall development of a nation.
  - Sahlberg, P. (2011). PISA in Finland: An education miracle or an obstacle to change?. *CEPS Journal: Center for Educational Policy Studies Journal, 1*(3), 119.

▶ Consider the two approaches: drawing from established work and constructing a conceptual framework. How would you establish the theoretical foundation for your research?

Drawing from established work	Constructing a conceptual framework
Who are the established theorists and scholars in your field? *What are theories and concepts emerging in the most recent literature?*	*What are the limitations of the existing theories and concepts?* *What are theories and concepts in other fields that could inform your research?*

▶ Using the inventory of language, write a few sentences to establish the theoretical foundation of your research.

10

Extensive Literature Review

 Opening Questions

- Thinking about your research timeline and the different stages of research and thesis writing, when do you begin the literature review process?
- How would you conduct a literature review?
- How would you best organize and present your literature review?

 In this chapter, you will···

Articulate the tasks and steps taken to complete a robust literature review.

Organize literature review content to effectively communicate your research aims and purposes.

Engaging in a thorough and comprehensive literature review is crucial for the success of a thesis and any academic writing endeavor. This process not only fosters the development of lifelong learning and self-directed research skills but also enables a deep understanding of the field, facilitating the identification of pertinent problems and the execution of original research. The construction of a robust literature review within a thesis is imperative, focusing on a specific issue or phenomenon to fortify the overall argument.

Neglecting to conduct an extensive literature review may lead to several pitfalls in academic research and thesis writing. The absence of a solid theoretical foundation is a common consequence (see Chapter 9 for details), where a researcher may only skim the surface of variable relationships or make hasty generalizations without considering the theoretical backgrounds. Additionally, inadequate organization and synthesis of prior research can result in presumptuous data collection, potentially duplicating previous studies. Failure to apply a problem-solving research method may result in research and thesis that lack clarity in terms of defining the problem and justifying the study that will be conducted. More importantly, the originality of your research may suffer as you may struggle to construct a convincing argument that highlights the unique contribution of your work.

Searching for and Documenting Relevant Literature

Before you begin searching for literature, make sure your research problem(s) and question(s) are clearly defined (see Chapter 8). The literature review process often begins with the identification of the problem and continues throughout the process of establishing a theoretical foundation until you reach the stage of writing a literature review section. As you survey previous research, you will recognize the gap in research, gain a more in-depth understanding of related theories and concepts, and see how these connect to your research. To guide this process, consider the following questions:

1. *Identify keywords:* What are the key terms, concepts, and words used in previous research related to your topic?

2. *Broad reading*: What problems were addressed in previous research, and how were these problems approached and resolved?

3. *Gather and collect*: What empirical research studies have attempted to answer questions or address problems similar to yours?

4. *Close reading*: What were the research questions, theoretical frameworks, methodologies, and findings/results in these studies?

5. *Analyze through the theoretical lens*: What studies employed your chosen theoretical lens, and how are these studies relevant to or inform your research?

6. *Address the gap*: What did previous research uncover, and what aspects remain unexplored or inadequately addressed?

7. *Reiterate the originality of your research*: HHHHow does your research differ from others, and what legitimate reasons emerge from the reviewed literature to justify your research?

By addressing these questions, you can lay a solid foundation for your research and thesis, ensuring a well−informed, original, and compelling contribution to the academic discourse.

Unfavorable Literature Review

A high−quality literature review requires rather advanced knowledge and writing skills, which may feel overwhelming to novice researchers and writers. It is also not a straightforward process since, as mentioned earlier, the literature review process begins at the initial stage of establishing a problem. Writing a literature review, to some extent, does not end until you wrap up your thesis writing. There are, however, some common mistakes and errors novice writers and researchers should be cautious of when writing a literature review.

Over−reliance on (low−quality) sources: As mentioned in Chapter 6, over−reliance on sources and literature alone is unfavorable and a very common mistake made by novice writers. Because the researcher feels insecure about their knowledge and expertise in the subject, we observe writers speaking through the voice of the literature instead of having their own voice. When you rely on low−quality sources, the result is even worse. Bear in mind that blog posts, daily news articles, and opinion pieces often carry less credibility, lacking scholarly rigor found in peer−reviewed journals or books. Prioritize review of well−recognized, peer−reviewed, up−to−date journal articles, along with books from reputable academic publishers. Instead of repeating what they said in these sources, review and make your own unique interpretations as you write a literature review.

Lack of established/seminal literature: Weaker or unfavorable literature reviews may stem from overlooking seminal research done by established scholars—foundational works that initially introduced significant ideas or concepts within the field. These seminal works inform building the foundation of a field or discipline and should be acknowledged in a comprehensive literature review. For instance, in Kim's (2021) research on exploring elementary teacher candidates' professional identities as language teachers of ELLs, a subsequent time was spent outlining theories and approaches to teacher identity studies (see Figure 9). Identifying and situating your research in these seminal works can guide you in finding more reliable sources and solidifying your research purpose.

Lack of current literature: A common shortcoming in the literature viewers written by emerging scholars or novice writers is the absence of current literature. While acknowledging established scholars and seminal works is meaningful, a strong literature review incorporates recent research findings and current debates, demonstrating a comprehensive understanding of classic and contemporary studies. Keep in mind that thanks to the advent of technology enabling higher speed and efficiency to knowledge sharing, research published within the past 5−7 years is considered current literature, while research older than 8−10 years are recognized as old research. Because of this reason, it is also not advisable to rely on other scholars' literature review articles that often reviewed 10−15 years of research, which may not make relevant connections to your research questions or purposes.

Theories of Teacher Professional Identity

In order to explore teacher candidates' belief system and their potential transformation, scholars have proposed gaining an in−depth understanding of their developing professional identities as future teachers (Varghese et al., 2005)…Identity research can be characterized by four major perspectives, including (a) a psychosocial perspective, (b) an intersubjective perspective, (c) a storied perspective, and (d) a dialogical perspective (Smith & Sparkes, 2008)…

Psychosocial perspective: multiple inner worlds

In the psychosocial perspective, an individual and their inner world are stressed over social influences; that is, the internal cognitive or psychological structure from one's internalization of experiences is a focus of the interrogation…

Intersubjective perspective: individual and social identity

While the psychosocial perspective emphasizes the individual's internalized structure and their inner world, the intersubjective perspective pays attention to the individual's organized view of self in relation to others…

Storied perspective: cumulative resources of identity

In the storied perspective, identity is understood as an accumulation of narrative resources and, thus, pays attention to a person's self−narration of their socially situated identities…

Dialogical perspective: on−going social identity

The dialogical perspective puts the least emphasis on the individual and focuses more on the social aspect of identity… Following Sachs and Dialogical Self Theory scholars, this study approaches teacher professional identity as a developing framework for teachers to believe, view, understand, and reflect on the nature of their teaching profession.

Figure 9. Sample of Literature Review on Seminal Theorizations (Kim, 2021)

Lack of synthesis: This was emphasized many times in other chapters as well and holds particular importance. Unfortunately, this is the most common error made by novice writers and emerging scholars. It is a mistake to perceive a literature review as a mere summation of individual researcher's perspectives. The detailed account of "he said, she said" throughout the writing degrades the relevance of the research and oftentimes leads the readers to question the researcher's knowledge and expertise. A high–quality literature review should synthesize existing research to illustrate how these various pieces interconnect. The important aspect is that these pieces are not only interconnected with each other but seamlessly connect to your research. Think of a literature review as a jigsaw puzzle where each puzzle piece represents an individual research article. The key is that you should know the final complete picture established in order to piece each puzzle piece; otherwise, the only job you can do is lay out individual puzzle pieces on the table.

Irrelevant or unrelated content: Aligned with the jigsaw puzzle analogy where you need the final picture figured out before you put together the puzzle pieces, if you include puzzle pieces that do not belong to complete the whole puzzle, you cannot present a completed pieced–together puzzle. As mentioned earlier, this commonly happens when novice writers rely heavily on one or two literature review pieces instead of doing the groundwork themselves. It is essential to align the literature review with your research aims, purposes, and research questions. Because the primary goal of a literature review is to provide a foundation and rationale for the research questions, the content should be relevant to and focused on the purpose of your research. As you navigate through the literature review process, constantly refer back to your research aims, purposes, and questions.

Organization of a Literature Review

A literature review, similar to any other genre of academic writing, maintains the structure and organization with an introduction, main body, and conclusion. It is crucial to allocate enough time to structure the main body of your literature review. The main body of your literature review will represent the central message and set the tone of your research. There are various ways to approach structuring the main body of your literature review, such as organizing the content chronologically, thematically, based on the methodology used, or according to the arguments. A well−articulated and well−grounded research should also include an in−depth literature review of the theoretical or conceptual framework.

A chronological approach means the sources are organized based on the year of publication. This may be helpful, especially in cases where you need to illustrate the historical developments of certain theories, concepts, or research trends. A limitation of this approach, however, is that it may inhibit the continuity and coherence of your arguments.

Organizing based on themes may allow more coherence in your arguments. This means as you review literature, you are focusing on the overarching topics to present themes and sub−themes as they emerge. This approach can be helpful to present an overview of the ongoing debates relevant to your research aims and purposes. Additionally, a thematic approach allows you to shift easily between chronological periods within each sub−theme section.

A methodological approach is common, especially in thesis writings, because of the following methodology section that allows a rather logical transition. A methodological approach is often utilized in the introduction of a literature review as the researcher states how a particular topic or subject has been studied in certain common perspectives and methods. This approach can form the basis of the discussion in main body to illustrate the methods used in previous research and the subsequent results or findings.

An argument−based approach can be another option to organize source coherently. This approach naturally enables you to synthesize sources and add your voice in the literature review as you present key debates and convey a message in the manner to which you organize them. The approach also allows flexibility for you to introduce additional theories or literature outside or related to the subject in order to support your research goals.

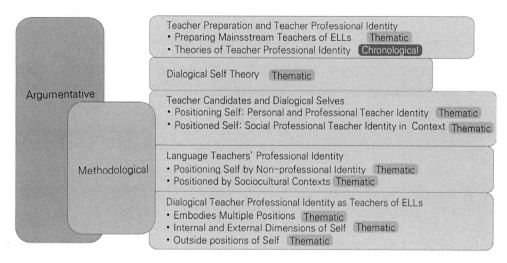

Figure 10. Sample Literature Review Organization (Kim, 2021)

Organizing the main body of your literature review is not a straightforward process; it is an iterative process that takes multiple attempts or arranging, re−arranging, and incorporating multiple approaches. These approaches are also interwoven and interconnected (see Figure 11), as you can witness from the sample organization of a literature review from Kim's (2021) dissertation. Although certain sections are labeled as using a thematic or chronological approach, in reality, thematic and argumentative approaches, as well as a chronological approach, are employed when the texts are merged into a final report of a literature review.

 Writing About⋯ The Problem

A few language functions that might help your literature review writing are: providing examples, referencing sources/reporting others' work, and signaling transition.

PROVIDING EXAMPLES

Providing examples refers to a strategic use of specific instances, cases, or illustrations to support, clarify, or exemplify a point, argument, or concept. This is an essential function to enhance the overall quality and effectiveness of your literature review, as you can utilize the examples to support the readers' understanding and reinforce your research aims and goals.

- **Various approaches have been used to** approximate the process of teaching linguistically diverse students and to promote moving beyond deficit perspectives of these students and their learning. **Efforts include** modeling linguistically responsive actions to gain familiarity with students' varied linguistic and academic backgrounds (Lucas, Villegas, & Freedson−Gonzalez, 2008) and role−playing emergent bilingual learners in a mathematics lesson taught in Portuguese with and without language scaffolds (de Oliveira, 2011).
    - Athanases, S. & Wong, J. W. (2018). Learning from analyzing linguistically diverse students' work: A contribution of preservice teacher inquiry. The Educational Forum, 82(2), 191−207

- Grammar accuracy is the primary criterion by which they assessed a person's command of language. **As an example**, Emily's comment was that whatever "roughness" is present in an international pal's writing is labeled as nonstandard grammar.
    - Hilliker, S. & Laletina, A. (2018). What do mainstream teachers think, know, and think they know about English language learners? *NYS TESOL Journal, 5*(1), 30−50.

- This disjunction between research and practice stems from practical factors (e.g., too few bilingual teachers), ideological factors (e.g., opposition to languages other than English in schools), and federal policy. **For instance,** the No Child Left Behind Act of 2001 (NCLB, 2003) required schools to monitor the academic performance of ELLs through state standardized tests.
    - Lucas, T., Strom, K., Bratkovich, M., & Wnuk, J. (2018). Inservice preparation for mainstream teachers of English language learners: A review of the empirical literature. *The Educational Forum, 82*(2),

156−173.

- **In another example**, Campbell (2008) reported that at the University of Washington, Seattle, where interns participated in mediated instruction in their math certification program, they developed a deeper understanding of the promoted teaching practices and were more successful in enacting the practices in diverse urban secondary schools.

  - Zeichner, K. (2010). Rethinking the connections between campus courses and field experiences in college− and university−based teacher education. *Journal of Teacher Education, 61*(1−2), 89−99.

- Some teacher educators, though, have taken advantage of the school location and have strategically connected their school−based methods course to the practices and expertise of teachers in those schools. **One example of this is** the work during the past few years at the University of Washington, Seattle, where methods instructors in elementary and secondary teacher education have held a portion of their courses in a K−12 partner school.

  - Zeichner, K. (2010). Rethinking the connections between campus courses and field experiences in college−and university−based teacher education. *Journal of Teacher Education, 61*(1−2), 89−99.

REFERENCING SOURCES/REPORTING OTHERS' WORK

Referencing sources/reporting others' work involves the writing practices of citing and acknowledging the works, ideas, or findings of other's research work. As you write your literature review, you should provide specific details about the sources you consulted in the citation style you are expected to use in your discipline (i.e., APA, MLA, Chicago, etc.). This function is utilized constantly in your research and thesis writing, which means you need a variety of language options at your disposal to diversify your expression.

- **Studies have found that** translanguaging is a social practice that goes beyond classroom interactions and that it includes all metadiscursive regimes that are performed by all multilingual speakers in their everyday way of making sense of the world around them (García, 2009; Wei, 2011). **To explain this phenomenon,** García (2009) **uses** a metaphor of an all−terrain car that has wheels that extend, contract, flex, and stretch while making movements that are irregular on 'an uneven ground' (García, 2009: 45).
  - Makalela, L. (2015). Translanguaging as a vehicle for epistemic access: Cases for reading comprehension and multilingual interactions. *Per Linguam: a Journal of Language Learning= Per Linguam: Tydskrif vir Taalaanleer, 31*(1), 15−29.

- In education, King (2004) **draws on** Wynter's scholarship **to propose a** "deciphering" form of culture−centered knowledge that moves beyond relations of domination, masked by calls for unity, toward conditions of autonomy where "differences are not suppressed or ranked" (p. 357). **She defines** culture−centered knowledge **as** the "thought, perception, and belief structures" that contribute to generating "the coherence of a referent social framework" required "to secure the loyalty, motivated participation, and relevant consciousness of its subjects (adherents)" (p. 357).
  - North, C. E. (2006). More than words? Delving into the substantive meaning (s) of "social justice" in education. *Review of Educational Research, 76*(4), 507−535.

- Cochran−Smith (2005) **argues that** social, intellectual, and organisational contexts shape the learning of teachers enrolled in preparation programmes and therefore attitudes regarding diversity can be addressed through the reconceptualisation of teacher education programmes.
  - Cardona Moltó, M. C., Florian, L., Rouse, M. & Stough, L. M. (2010) Attitudes to diversity: a cross-cultural study of education students in Spain,

England and the United States, European Journal of Teacher Education, 33(3), 245−264, DOI: 10.1080/02619768.2010.495771

- "To be human one must have a story," Nigerian writer Chinua Achebe once **said**. "It's one of the things humans do. Not just hear a story, but tell a story," (Sengupta 2010), **he further explained**.
    - Pulitano, E. (2013). In liberty's shadow: the discourse of refugees and asylum seekers in critical race theory and immigration law/politics. *Identities, 20*(2), 172−189.

- **Openly condemning** the racialised standards of the ideological War on Terror, **Danticat describes such** inhuman treatment of Haitian refugees **as** the 'most horrifying distortion of the American dream, which is now only made up of prison nightmares' (2004, p. 172).
    - Pulitano, E. (2013). In liberty's shadow: the discourse of refugees and asylum seekers in critical race theory and immigration law/politics. *Identities, 20*(2), 172−189.

- Emler and Frazer (1999) **explain that** educational attainment indirectly affects political outcomes by determining one's social status and network, which then affect a person's attitudes towards war. The role of educational attainment and institutions, however, can be eclipsed by values instilled by one's family and community.
    - Shafiq, M. N. & Ross, K. (2010). Educational attainment and attitudes towards war in Muslim countries contemplating war: The cases of Jordan, Lebanon, Pakistan, and Turkey. *Journal of Development Studies, 46*(8), 1424−1441.

- Moreover, Hefner and Zaman (2007) **present** qualitative research from a number of Muslim countries **showing that** most madrassas do not subscribe to fundamentalist and intolerant views.

- Shafiq, M. N. & Ross, K. (2010). Educational attainment and attitudes towards war in Muslim countries contemplating war: The cases of Jordan, Lebanon, Pakistan, and Turkey. *Journal of Development Studies, 46*(8), 1424−1441.

- Ben−Porath (2006) **suggests that** during wartime, schools in democracies emphasise **what she calls** 'belligerent citizenship,' focusing on patriotism and national unity.
    - Shafiq, M. N. & Ross, K. (2010). Educational attainment and attitudes towards war in Muslim countries contemplating war: The cases of Jordan, Lebanon, Pakistan, and Turkey. *Journal of Development Studies, 46*(8), 1424−1441.

- **As** Gillborn (1997b) **notes** This is a powerful technique. First, it assumes that there are no genuine arguments against the chosen position; any opposing views are thereby positioned as false, insincere or self−serving. Second, the technique presents the speaker as someone brave or honest enough to speak the (previously) unspeakable. Hence, the moral high ground is assumed and opponents are further denigrated (p. 353).
    - Apple, M. (2001). Comparing neo−liberal projects and inequality in education. *Comparative Education, 37*(4), 409−423.

- **As Roger Dale reminds us,** 'the market' acts as a metaphor rather than an explicit guide for action. It is not denotative, but connotative. Thus, it must itself be 'marketed' to those who will exist in it and live with its effects [quoted in Menter et al. (1997, p. 27)].
    - Apple, M. (2001). Comparing neo−liberal projects and inequality in education. *Comparative Education, 37*(4), 409−423.

- Indeed, Finland is often used as a model of successful reform and strong performance in education. "As societies move beyond the age of low−skill standardization," **writes** Andy Hargreaves, "Finland contains essential lessons for nations that aspire, educationally and economically, to be successful and sustainable knowledge societies" (Hargreaves et al., 2008, p. 92).

- Sahlberg, P. (2011). PISA in Finland: An education miracle or an obstacle to change?. *CEPS Journal: Center for Educational Policy Studies Journal, 1*(3), 119.

SIGNALING TRANSITION

Signaling transition in academic writing is another useful linguistic function you need to utilize throughout your research and thesis writing. This function helps to guide readers smoothly from one idea, paragraph, or section to another. By doing so, you are indicating shifts in focus, introducing new topics, summarizing information, or highlighting connections between different parts, which gives a logical flow to the text. This ensures the readers follow the progression of your ideas and enriches the coherence and organization of your writing.

- **The above studies point to** the gap between the orientation to language of the state (as expressed in its language policy) and the orientation to language in everyday contexts. The plurilingual communicative practices we see in schools and social domains point to a different orientation to language contact. While the policy statements envision the relationship between languages in one way, everyday practices at the ground level point to a different orientation. **We will turn to this distinction below.**
  - Canagarajah, S. & Ashraf, H. (2013).Multilingualism and education in South Asia: Resolving policy/practice dilemmas. *Annual Review of Applied Linguistics, 33*, 258–285.

- Based on the plurilingual tradition **described in the last section,** we can understand why Khubchandani (2008) was critical of policies based on "privileges and parity." He favored a pedagogy that facilitates functional proficiency in different languages for different purposes.

- Canagarajah, S. & Ashraf, H. (2013). Multilingualism and education in South Asia: Resolving policy/practice dilemmas. *Annual Review of Applied Linguistics, 33*, 258–285.

- **As discussed in the Introduction,** the conventional view is that educated people are more likely to support peaceful perspectives, such as pacifism or just war theory.
  - Shafiq, M. N. & Ross, K. (2010). Educational attainment and attitudes towards war in Muslim countries contemplating war: The cases of Jordan, Lebanon, Pakistan, and Turkey. *Journal of Development Studies, 46*(8), 1424–1441.

- These claims, both about what is happening inside schools and about larger sets of power relations, are supported by even more recent synthetic analyses of the overall results of marketised models. This research on the effects of the tense but still effective combination of neo−liberal and neo−conservative policies examines the tendencies internationally by comparing what has happened in a number of nations−for example, the USA, England and Wales, Australia, and New Zealand−where this combination has been increasingly powerful. The results confirm the arguments I have made here. **Let me rehearse some of the most significant and disturbing findings of such research.**
  - Apple, M. (2001). Comparing neo−liberal projects and inequality in education. *Comparative Education, 37*(4), 409–423.

- Since it is impossible to conclude whether there has been progress in student learning in general, **let us look at** some school subjects that have been included in international studies individually.
  - Sahlberg, P. (2011). PISA in Finland: An education miracle or an obstacle to change?. CEPS *Journal: Center for Educational Policy Studies Journal, 1*(3), 119.

- As mentioned previously, there are three main phases in this study. The first one, which underlies this paper, focuses on identifying teachers" perceptions of their own role inside the EFL classroom. A second stage will be to identify students" beliefs regarding the role of the teacher. The third phase will include an analysis of what institutional documents from two Mexican universities foresee as the role of the teacher. In what follows, we will present a review of previous research carried out, both inside and outside of Mexico.

  - Narvaez Trejo, O. M. & Heffington, D. (2011). Exploring Teachers' Perceptions of their Role in the EFL Classroom: Some Considerations. *Memorias del VI foro de estudios en lenguas internacional (FEL 2010)*. Retrieved from: http://www.uv.mx/personal/onarvaez/files/2012/09/Exploring −Teachers−perceptions−of−their−Role−in−the−EFL−Classroom.pdf

- As previously argued, reference is made to the universal characteristics (etic properties), cultural (emic properties), and individual characteristics of the phenomena or concept studied in trans−cultural research.

  - Cardona Moltó, M. C., Florian, L., Rouse, M. & Stough, L. M. (2010) Attitudes to diversity: a cross-cultural study of education students in Spain, England and the United States, European Journal of Teacher Education, 33(3), 245−264, DOI: 10.1080/02619768.2010.495771

- In the remainder of this essay, then, I explore some of the tensions within theories of recognition and redistribution that bear on approaches to education for social justice.

  - North, C. E. (2006). More than words? Delving into the substantive meaning (s) of "social justice" in education. *Review of Educational Research*, 76(4), 507−535.

Reflection Questions

▸ What did you learn about research ethics? What are aspects you have not considered or anticipated before?

▸ What are the actions you need to take in your specific research project in order to conduct ethical research?

11

Beyond Research Methodology as a Tool

 Opening Questions

- What is your understanding of research methodology?
- What content should be included in the research methodology section?

 In this chapter, you will···

- Explain the difference between research methodology and research methods.
- Illustrate the relationships between research philosophy, methodology, and methods.

Research methodology is often perceived and used interchangeably with research methods. However, these are two different concepts that require careful thought and distinctions. A research methodology, grounded in philosophical principles and perspectives, is a broader concept than a research method, which is merely a tool used in research.

Let us use an analogy of teaching to distinguish between research methodologies and methods. If you think about a teacher concentrating solely on the 'teacher methods,' it is more likely that they miss the essence of effective instruction. For example, the teacher employs a think−pair−share activity in every lesson without a clear understanding of its purpose or why it is chosen over other alternative activities. The teacher's simple lack of foundational principles in the implementation of an activity may easily result in a fruitless time−killing strategy that does not allow students an opportunity to learn something.

The teaching analogy extends to the importance of establishing one's teaching philosophy—teaching influenced by Vygotskian principles will diverge significantly from that guided by Piagetian principles. Just as every teacher requires a guiding principle and philosophy to inform their teaching methods, researchers need a robust methodology. What were the guiding principles of the methodology, that led the researcher to consider specific research methods?

Understanding Research Methodologies

When researchers concentrate exclusively on methods without a guiding methodology, pitfalls emerge. Referring back to our teacher analogy, a teacher's oversight of neglecting the underlying learning theory may hinder the ability to deliver optimal teaching. Furthermore, a teacher's fixation on teaching methods can lead to constantly seeking technical solutions to a problem rather than taking the time to consider educational philosophies or learning theories to guide them. This 'methods−fetish' may impede student learning and hinder the teacher's professional development, as the absence of guiding principles leaves educators ill−equipped to navigate new challenges or dilemmas. Research methodologies are not different. It is often observed that novice scholars choose 'trendy' research methods or 'buzzword' research concepts or theories without properly taking the time to consider their research methodologies. Scholars have cautioned against such an excessive focus on methods in isolation:

Bartolome, L. (1994). Beyond the methods fetish: Toward a humanizing pedagogy. *Harvard Educational Review*, 64(2), 173−195.

Bartolome, L. I. (1996). Beyond the methods fetish: Toward a humanizing pedagogy. *Breaking free: The transformative power of critical pedagogy*, 229252.

It is essential for researchers to consider their ontology and epistemology as they construct the methodology for their research. Figure 10 depicts how ontology and epistemology set the foundation for research methodology, theory, and methods. Your ontological and epistemological perspectives form a comprehensive understanding of how knowledge is perceived and our position in relation to it, along with the methodological approaches employed to uncover or understand it. Recognizing these philosophical assumptions not only enhances the quality of research but also fosters the researcher's creativity. As you write your thesis, you are expected to articulate these philosophical foundations.

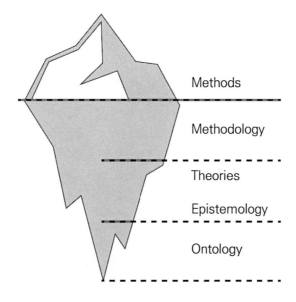

Figure 11. Conceptualization of Research Methodology

Research Paradigms: Ontology and Epistemology

ONTOLOGY

Ontology and epistemology are important research philosophical assumptions you need to know and subsequently explain in your methodology section. Ontology refers to the assumptions we have about reality and truth. Ontological assumptions grapple with the fundamental characteristics, origins, and observable phenomena. Simply put, researchers might be more inclined to believe in objective truths; subjective truths fall somewhere in between the two ends of the spectrum. It is critical to clarify your assumptions about the nature of reality and the fundamental aspects of the phenomena you are studying before you begin your research and thesis writing. Consider whether you believe in an objective reality that exists independently of human perception or if reality is shaped by individual experiences. The following questions might help you to gain some clarification:

- What is the nature of truth and reality?
- What exists? How can you describe its existence?

Ontology is concerned with the question of whether 'beings' or social entities should be regarded as objective or subjective. In the context of research and thesis writing, you need to determine whether the world exists independently of the social realm or if social phenomena are shaped by the perceptions and actions of individuals within that realm.

EPISTEMOLOGY

In conjunction with ontology, it is crucial for a researcher to reflect on the sources and processes through which knowledge is acquired. Consider your stance on whether knowledge is primarily derived from empirical evidence, social interactions, intuition, or a combination of these. Additionally, contemplate how you perceive others engage in the construction of knowledge.

- What is the nature of knowledge, and what are you trying to uncover?

- How can people claim to know anything at all?
- How was knowledge constructed, and how do you believe others construct knowledge?
- What does it mean to know something?

By contemplating these questions, your research questions and methods can be more refined and strongly grounded in research philosophies, strengthening the logical argument in your research. Research methodologies and methods are intricately connected, as research methodologies embody epistemologies. If your research methodologies and methods are disconnected from epistemologies, the claims and knowledge generated from your research can be compromised. Consider research methods as streamlined, purpose−specific epistemologies. The following Figure 12 depicts commonly known research paradigms corresponding to specific ontology, epistemology, and methodology.

PARADIGMS	ONTOLOGY	EPISTEMOLOGY	METHODOLOGY	METHOD
Positivism	External, objective, and independent view of social actors	Measurable reality	Experimental, quantitative research	Sampling, survey, focus group, statistical analysis, scaling
Pragmatism	External and multiple view of reality that is assumed to be renegotiated, debated, and interpreted	Best measured through problem solving. Underlying aim is change	Mixed*method, action research	Combination of quantitative and quilitative methods, data miming expert review, physical prototype
Subjectivism	Subjective, multiple, reality	Knowledge construction perceived as a matter of perspective	Discourse, archaeology, genealogy research	Autoehtnogrphy, semiotics, literacy analysis
Interpretivism/ Constructivism	Subjective, multiple, and socially constructed view of reality that is socially constructed	Interpreted reality through a discovery of underlying meaning	Ethnographic, grounded theory, phenomenological, heuristic research	Interview, obsercation, case study, lkfe history, narrative

Figure 12. Common Research Paradigms: Ontology, Epistemology, and Methodology

Methodologies, Theories, and Research Methods

THEORIES/THEORETICAL PERSPECTIVE

In the discussion of research paradigms, ontologies, and epistemologies, theoretical considerations are not always included as these may overlap with methodologies. Depending on the research paradigm and design, theoretical perspectives can also have less to weigh in compared to methodological choices. Theories and theoretical perspectives also overlap with epistemology as they align with epistemological approaches to understanding the nature of knowledge construction. Theories are typically in pursuit of answering the following questions:

- What approach can you use to get knowledge or know something?
- How can you interpret the world and knowledge through the lens that aligns with your perceptions of reality and knowledge construction?

Depending on your theoretical perspectives of viewing what constitutes knowledge, along with specific ways of producing knowledge, your methodological approach may look very different. Some examples of theoretical perspectives are:

- Positivism
- Post—positivism
- Interpretivism (phenomenology, hermeneutics)
- Postmodernism
- Structuralism
- Post—structuralism
- Marxism
- Feminism

As mentioned earlier, because of the overlaps in the terms and concepts such as positivism or interpretivism, theoretical perspectives are often understood as part of research paradigms or methodologies. It is important to be aware that the purpose and guiding questions are different in each approach, meaning, as one views reality in a positivist approach, the approach one takes to acquire this singular truth may entail a post−positivist approach where one is careful of the interpretations and assumptions people make. In essence, a theoretical perspective is a philosophical stance you take that shapes your methodology, offering a way to establish your research context, logic, and criteria.

METHODOLOGY

Methodology is the process you employ to identify and substantiate your argument, opinion, or belief—therefore, research aims. The methodology is where everything connects to one specific point. Your methodology is informed and shaped by your ontology, epistemology, and theoretical perspectives. Your methodology also needs to align with your research aims, purposes, and questions. You need to evaluate and select a research design (methodology) that aligns with your philosophical stance on knowledge. Ask yourself these questions:

- What is the best way to investigate the problem based on your epistemology and theoretical perspectives on knowledge construction?
- How do you go about finding out the knowledge or reality you are seeking?

For example, if you value experiential knowledge, qualitative methods might be more suitable, while a belief in objective truths may lead you toward quantitative approaches. Bear in mind that research methodologies involve philosophical underpinnings, while research methods encompass very specific ways of collecting and analyzing your research data. Research methodology focuses on how you acquire knowledge and approach the information−gathering process to address your research problem. It is a systematic way in which you explore and uncover knowledge.

RESEARCH METHODS

Your research methods are specific data collection and analysis tools that resonate with your overall research philosophy. Consider the appropriateness of methods such as surveys, experiments, case studies, or interviews based on your epistemological and methodological foundation. You also need to ensure that your chosen methods align with the overarching framework guiding your study. The following questions should be answered as you choose the research methods:

- What is the best tool to collect and analyze the data based on your ontology, epistemology, theoretical perspective, and methodology?
- What techniques should you use to find out answers to your research questions?

The data collection methods you choose will be contingent on the type of data you plan to collect (i.e., qualitative or quantitative data). For quantitative data, it is common to rely on instruments such as surveys, data from analytics software, or pre-existing datasets. In qualitative data collection, typical forms of data entail interviews, focus groups, participant observation, and ethnography.

The data analysis methods, also determined by the type of data you collect, should align with your epistemology and methodology. In your research and thesis writing, you are expected to specifically outline how you analyze your data once collected. For qualitative studies, typically well-known analysis methods are content analysis, thematic analysis, and discourse analysis. In quantitative studies, common methods are descriptive statistics and inferential statistical analyses.

Writing the Research Methodology/Research Design Section

As usual, the research methodology section should be organized with an introduction, main body, and conclusion. The main body typically includes a few key elements: Research philosophy, methodology/research design, research questions or hypotheses, data collection methods, and data analysis methods. As you construct your research methodology section, consider the following questions.

- What led you to select this research topic?
- Considering your ontological and epistemological assumptions, how might you approach your research problem?
- In previous studies, how was the theoretical perspective employed in

investigating this research topic/problem?

- To align with your beliefs and assumptions, how can you structure the results and findings of previous studies on this topic?

- Based on your ontological, epistemological, and theoretical underpinnings, how can the research design aid in exploring this research topic?

- What tools are more effective for applying your theoretical lens and analyzing your topic?

- What contribution does your research aim to make to the field?

Quantitative	Qualitative	Mixed-method
Introduction	Introduction	Introduction
Research perspective	Research perspective	Research perspective
Research design	Research design	Research design
Research questions	Research questions	Research questions
Research procedure	Research context	Research context
Population & sample	Participant selection	Research procedure
Instrumentation	Data collection	Sample
Data collection	Data analysis	Data collection
data analysis	Researcher positionality	Data analysis
Trustworthiness	Trustworthiness	Trustworthiness
Conclusion	Conclusion	Conclusion

Figure 13. Organization of the Methodology/Research Design Section

The specific organization of your methodology/research design section may look different depending on the methodology you choose. The following are commonly included sections in a research methodology section (specifically in research thesis writings).

 Writing About⋯ The Problem

Writing the research methodology section, especially in thesis writing, is a challenging and extensive writing process. It requires comprehensive knowledge of your research field, philosophical orientations, and methodological approaches. Furthermore, it requires proficient writing skills to articulate complex philosophy, paradigms, theories, and methods while carefully navigating the mine to avoid sounding like a parrot repeating everything said in the research methodology textbooks. Some functions that might help you in the process of crafting a research methodology section are: making claims/objections /arguments, establishing cause and effect, and showing use of cautious language.

MAKING CLAIMS/OBJECTIONS/ARGUMENTS

Making claims, objections, or arguments is the consistent underlying purpose of academic and research writing. You need to assert a position, present a viewpoint, or express a perspective on a particular topic or issue. As you articulate your research philosophy, stance, and assumptions, this particular function becomes more important.

- **Certainly**, there has been conceptual work on, for example, the impact of peacekeepers on state sovereignty; on 'peace maintenance'; and on the Neo−Grotian legitimacy of 'saving strangers'. **But** the cartography of much of the writing on this issue has been determined by problem−solving imperatives.

    - Pugh, M. (2004). Peacekeeping and critical theory. *International peacekeeping, 11*(1), 39−58.

- Through the use of narratives, or counter−stories, marginalised groups who have never been able to legitimise their experiences within the master story of white supremacy bring cohesiveness and strength to their communities. More important, they challenge the fundamental tenets of hegemonic discourse by rejecting colour−blindness and exposing racism as a determining factor in the inequities of American society. **Yet** storytelling as an empowering tool for asylum seekers has been largely overlooked by CRT scholarship. **Despite** ongoing attention brought to questions of immigration, asylum **has remained** a sort of an uncharted territory in the research agenda of critical race theorists. The fact that some of the most popular CRT readers, the same that are used in undergraduate courses across the country, **do not even include** a section on asylum **is indicative of** this scholarship void.

- Pulitano, E. (2013). In liberty's shadow: the discourse of refugees and asylum seekers in critical race theory and immigration law/politics. *Identities, 20*(2), 172−189.

• Like the 'huddled masses' chanted in Emma Lazarus's (1883) famous poem, and whose verses are affixed to the bottom pedestal of the Statue of Liberty, immigrants and asylum seekers continue to arrive in America having embraced the mythic tale of this country as the land of equity and justice for all. Soon, **however**, they realise that the ideological narrative inscribed in America's iconic symbol of freedom and hope **is belied** by a reality of oppressive immigration policies that in most cases results in racial and national discrimination. They realise that post−9/11 America **does not really** want all of the 'tired masses yearning to breathe free', **but** only a selected few.

- Pulitano, E. (2013). In liberty's shadow: the discourse of refugees and asylum seekers in critical race theory and immigration law/politics. *Identities, 20*(2), 172−189.

• **Despite** these concerns, **there is no empirical evidence** from developing countries demonstrating how ordinary adults' attitudes towards war vary with their educational attainment. The main reason for the lack of empirical research is that, until very recently, surveys on political attitudes of ordinary adults were not systematically collected in developing countries (Tessler and Jamal, 2006; Evans and Rose, 2007).

- Shafiq, M. N. & Ross, K. (2010). Educational attainment and attitudes towards war in Muslim countries contemplating war: The cases of Jordan, Lebanon, Pakistan, and Turkey. *Journal of Development Studies, 46*(8), 1424−1441.

• In addition to ongoing skirmishes with Israel, Lebanon has also experienced conflict with its neighbour Syria, which occupied the country in 1976 as part of an Arab peacekeeping force and left only in 2005, after dominating Lebanese politics for nearly 30 years (Fattah, 2005). **Nevertheless**, Syrian involvement in the country has not ended: for example, Syrian actors continue to smuggle arms into Lebanese territory to equip Hezbollah in the fight against Israel (UN News Center, 2008).

- Shafiq, M. N. & Ross, K. (2010). Educational attainment and attitudes towards war in Muslim countries contemplating war: The cases of Jordan, Lebanon, Pakistan, and Turkey. *Journal of Development Studies*, *46*(8), 1424−1441.

- Gary McCulloch **argues** that the nature of the historical images of schooling has changed. Dominant imagery of education as being 'safe, domesticated, and progressive' (that is, as leading towards progress and social/personal improvement) has shifted to become 'threatening, estranged, and regressive' (McCulloch, 1997, p. 80). The past is no longer the source of stability, but a mark of failure, disappointment, and loss. This is seen most vividly in the attacks on the 'progressive orthodoxy' that supposedly now reigns supreme in classrooms in many nations (Hirsch, 1996; Ravitch, 2000).
  - Apple, M. (2001). Comparing neo−liberal projects and inequality in education. *Comparative Education, 37*(4), 409−423.

- It should go without saying that these dynamics will have their own rhythms and specificities in different nations with different histories of their articulations and interactions. Indeed, **I would argue that** how these interact is one of the most important issues of research in comparative education.
  - Apple, M. (2001). Comparing neo−liberal projects and inequality in education. *Comparative Education, 37*(4), 409−423.

- **Although** it is difficult to compare students' learning outcomes today with those in 1980, **some evidence of** progress of student learning in Finland **can** be offered using IEA and PISA surveys recorded since the 1970s (Kupari & Valijarvi, 2005; Martin et al., 2000; Robitaille & Garden, 1989).

- Sahlberg, P. (2011). PISA in Finland: An education miracle or an obstacle to change?. *CEPS Journal: Center for Educational Policy Studies Journal, 1*(3), 119.

- As Finland attracts global attention today due to its high−performing education system, **it is worth asking whether there has really been** any progress in the performance of its students since the 1970s. If such progress can be reliably identified in any terms, the question then becomes: What factors might be behind successful education reform? When education systems are compared internationally **it is important to have a broader perspective than** just student achievement.

  - Sahlberg, P. (2011). PISA in Finland: An education miracle or an obstacle to change?. *CEPS Journal: Center for Educational Policy Studies Journal, 1*(3), 119.

- It is important to note that any effects that teaching may have on these **results** in given education systems **have been influenced primarily by** education policies and reforms implemented in the 1990s, **not by the** most recent education reforms.

  - Sahlberg, P. (2011). PISA in Finland: An education miracle or an obstacle to change?. *CEPS Journal: Center for Educational Policy Studies Journal, 1*(3), 119.

- **It is also worth noting that there is growing criticism among** Finnish educators **about the ways** that students' performance and success in education systems **are determined by using only** the test scores from academic student assessments. **Many would like to see a broader scope of** student learning considered in these assessments, **such as** learning−to−learn skills, social competences, self−awareness or creativity.

- Sahlberg, P. (2011). PISA in Finland: An education miracle or an obstacle to change?. CEPS *Journal: Center for Educational Policy Studies Journal, 1*(3), 119.

- Another major source of challenge to the model of multilingualism informing the language−in−education policy in India and Pakistan is the communicative practices in social institutions, schools, and everyday life. **Rather than being** separated and enjoying their own autonomous domain, the languages (including English) are coming into contact in hybrid forms of communication.

  - Canagarajah, S. & Ashraf, H. (2013).Multilingualism and education in South Asia: Resolving policy/practice dilemmas. *Annual Review of Applied Linguistics, 33*, 258–285.

ESTABLISHING CAUSE AND EFFECT

Establishing cause and effect refers to analyzing the causal relationship between two or more variables, events, phenomena, or concepts. While this writing function is useful when you are writing your research findings, it is also deemed important to utilize in the methodology writing. As you understand and make logical connections between your research philosophy and methodology, knowing how to write causal relationships will serve you well.

- **Because of this,** it is important that any analysis of the current play of forces surrounding conservative modernisation is aware of the fact that not only are such movements in constant motion, but once again we need to remember that they have a multitude of intersecting and contradictory dynamics including not only class, but race and gender as well (Arnot et al.,1999; Apple, 2000).

  - Apple, M. (2001). Comparing neo−liberal projects and inequality in education. *Comparative Education, 37*(4), 409−423.

- Markets are marketed, are made legitimate, by a depoliticising strategy. They are said to be natural and neutral, and governed by effort and merit. And those opposed to them are by definition, **hence**, also opposed to effort and merit. Markets, as well, are supposedly less subject to political interference and the weight of bureaucratic procedures. Plus, they are grounded in the rational choices of individual actors. **Thus**, markets and the guarantee of rewards for effort and merit are to be coupled together to produce 'neutral', yet positive, results (Menter et al., 1997, p. 27). Mechanisms, hence, must be put into place that give evidence of entrepreneurial efficiency and effectiveness. This coupling of markets and mechanisms for the generation of evidence of performance **is exactly what has occurred.**

- Apple, M. (2001). Comparing neo−liberal projects and inequality in education. *Comparative Education, 37*(4), 409−423.

- A national pilot programme on teacher induction was established in 2002 and has been extended on a gradual basis since its inception. Plans are currently afoot to extend the programme nationally and some progress has been made in the structure and design of induction seminars through the national education centre network. However participation is on a volunteer basis. **As a result**, unlike the majority of beginning professionals in other professions, new entrants to teaching in Ireland can be expected to assume a full teaching load with no designated time given over to allow for observation, team−teaching, reflection on practice, mentoring, all of the tenets of an effective induction experience (Abbott 2009; Draper and O'Brien 2006; Killeavy and Murphy 2006).

- Harford, J. (2010). Teacher education policy in Ireland and the challenges of the twenty-first century. *European Journal of Teacher Education, 33*(4), 349−360.

- Such inequalities between languages point to larger ideological conflicts in society. In both countries, the greater emphasis on English marks the tensions between the local needs and global trends. On the one hand, emphasis on learning through one's first languages is considered a learner's basic right; on the other hand, there is an acknowledgment that globalization creates a demand for English. This difference **has resulted in** creating a distinct hierarchical divide with all other languages that are indigenous to the subcontinent in spite of widespread multilingualism.

- Canagarajah, S. & Ashraf, H. (2013).Multilingualism and education in South Asia: Resolving policy/practice dilemmas. *Annual Review of Applied Linguistics, 33,* 258 285.

- The main focus of educational performance in education systems that benchmark their policies and practices internationally is on student achievement in literacy, mathematics and science. **Therefore,** many national education policies today look similar − they focus on higher standards and closing achievement gaps by rewarding teachers for successful accomplishment of these strategic goals.

  - Sahlberg, P. (2011). PISA in Finland: An education miracle or an obstacle to change?. *CEPS Journal: Center for Educational Policy Studies Journal, 1*(3), 119.

- For example, at the University of Helsinki, each year about 15% of students in the primary school teacher education programme specialise in teaching mathematics. This also allows them to teach mathematics in lower secondary schools. **As a consequence,** most primary schools in Finland have professionals who understand the nature of teaching and learning − and curriculum and assessment − in mathematics.

  - Sahlberg, P. (2011). PISA in Finland: An education miracle or an obstacle to change?. *CEPS Journal: Center for Educational Policy Studies Journal, 1*(3), 119.

- These university studies, as part of normal teacher education, have focused on building pedagogical content knowledge and understanding of scientific process in knowledge creation. **Thus**, the science curriculum in comprehensive school has been transformed from a traditional academic knowledge—based curriculum to an experimental and problem—oriented curriculum.

- Sahlberg, P. (2011). PISA in Finland: An education miracle or an obstacle to change?. *CEPS Journal: Center for Educational Policy Studies Journal, 1*(3), 119.

- Ironically, the success of Finnish education during the past three decades **is due to** forward—looking education policies and active learning from other countries' education reforms and innovations.
  - Sahlberg, P. (2011). PISA in Finland: An education miracle or an obstacle to change?. *CEPS Journal: Center for Educational Policy Studies Journal, 1*(3), 119.

SHOWING USE OF CAUTIOUS LANGUAGE

There are moments in academic writing when you want to convey a sense of careful consideration. Showing use of cautious language is intended to show your precision and humility in presenting information and making claims. The methodology section, as we discussed, is where everything connects and comes into one place. Thus, knowing how to express your thoughtfulness demonstrates your careful approach to complex research procedures.

- Teacher inquiry **may** support development of such knowledge from a focus on asking critical questions of teaching and learning with particular students.
  - Athanases, S. & Wong, J. W. (2018). Learning from analyzing linguistically diverse students' work: A contribution of preservice teacher inquiry. *The Educational Forum, 82*(2), 191—207

- PSTs of color have firsthand experience of growing up and learning as nondominant students and **may be more likely to** value knowledge and skills diverse students bring to the classroom.

- Athanases, S. Z., Banes, L. C., & Wong , J. W. (2015). Diverse language profiles: Leveraging resources of potential bilingual teachers of color. *Bilingual Research Journal, 38* (1), 65−87. doi: 10.1080/15235882.2015.10 17622

• **One approach that can** enable a deeper engagement with metalinguistic awareness and other issues at the heart of a diverse and democratic society is self−reflexive inquiry (Asher, 2007). **This can be** meaningful for monolingual and White PSTs, as well, given a reported lack of awareness on the part of these PSTs of themselves as cultural beings (Sleeter, 2008).

- Athanases, S. Z., Banes, L. C., & Wong , J. W. (2015). Diverse language profiles: Leveraging resources of potential bilingual teachers of color. *Bilingual Research Journal, 38* (1), 65−87. doi: 10.1080/15235882.2015.10 17622

• **Perhaps** collective teacher research efforts **could** fill the void of a shared professional knowledge base in teaching.

- Dana, N. F., Yendol−Hoppey, D., & Snow−Gerono (2006). Deconstructing inquiry in the professional development school: Exploring the domains and contents of teachers' questions. *Action in Teacher Education, 27*(4), 59−71.

• Further, **given** the limitations of the alternative program's structures for preparing novices (e.g., time, amount of supervision offered to novices while they worked with children), **we do not seek to** imply that results would necessarily neatly map onto preparation programs of different designs.

- Kavanagh, S. S. & Rainey, E. C. (2017). Learning to support adolescent literacy: Techer educator pedagogy and novice teacher take up in secondary English language arts teacher preparation. *American Educational Research Journal, 54*(5), 904–937.

Reflection Questions

▸ How did your understanding change regarding research methodology and methods?

▸ Reflect on the relation between research purpose, philosophy, and methods. Outline your research to visualize the connections.

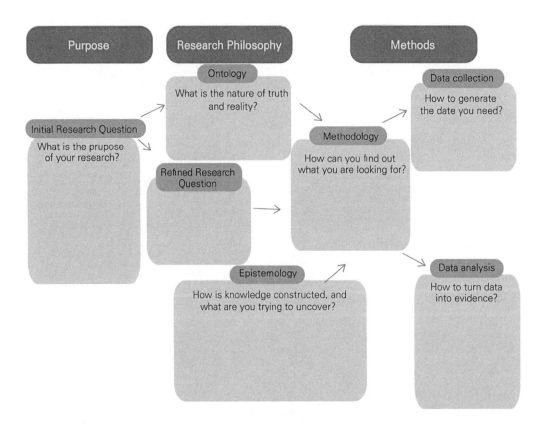

The Art of Presenting Findings and Results

 Opening Questions

- What are some key characteristics you noticed in other's presentation of findings or results?
- Why do you think presenting findings and results is described as a form of art?

 In this chapter, you will…

- Determine presentation methods for your research findings/results section.
- Practice crafting a findings/results section.

The findings or results section is where you report the findings of your research based on the methodology you applied to gather information. The results section should state the findings of the research arranged in a logical sequence without bias of interpretation. A section describing results should be particularly detailed if your thesis includes data generated from your research.

When formulating the results section, it is important to remember that the results of a study do not mean anything. Similar to a problem statement, there is no particular meaning or relevance to a simple reporting or description of the findings unless you craft a meaningful presentation of the findings. The art of articulating the results helps you to understand the problem from within, break it into pieces, and view the research problem from various perspectives.

Steps to Craft a Findings/Results Section

Although writing and presenting the findings section is an iterative process that would require multiple cycles of writing, reviewing, and rewriting, there are some basic steps you can take to get your writing process started.

Step 1: Systematically organize your findings/results focused on your research questions, aims, and purposes. Utilize subheadings to outline the structure of your findings/results section.

Step 2: Develop necessary data visuals (e.g., tables, figures, etc.) to illustrate your data effectively.

Step 3: Draft your findings/results section, maintaining clarity and precision. It is always a good idea to start by restating your research questions, aims, and purposes in the introduction. At the end of your findings/results section, consider adding a logical transition to the discussion section that will follow.

Step 4: Review, edit, and revise your draft. Do not be afraid to start all over if the first draft does not do justice to your findings/results. It is common to go through one or two iterative cycles before your findings/results are presented in the most effective way.

Ways to Present Data and Findings

Regardless of whether you designed quantitative, qualitative, or mixed−method research, the fact does not change that presenting the results to convey the interpretation accurately is the writer's responsibility. For example, suppose you read a news article titled "New discovery of a planet in our solar system." You open up the news article, and all there is is a snapshot of a round−ball−like object in a pitch−dark background—possibly a photo taken from a telescope. This leaves the majority of the work of interpreting the data left for the readers to find out. Simply providing numbers, charts, tables, or quotes and simply describing those data is similarly an irresponsible presentation of the findings. As a researcher and writer, it is your job to present thoughtfully interpreted findings in a manner that is easily understandable to even the readers who have no or limited knowledge in the subject area. There are a few approaches to make the presentation of your findings/results more accessible.

TABLES

Tables serve as an effective tool to provide an overview of the findings or results, whether you are presenting findings of qualitative research data or results of quantitative research data. The tables can include major themes, supporting evidence, and the meanings of each theme. In quantitative research results, tables, including graphs and figures, visualize the numbers in a more accessible manner. Even when utilizing such visuals, it is important to remember that you should never solely rely on visuals as a means of presenting your findings. You should contextualize and elucidate the findings in a narrative form as if you are telling a story with pictures.

THEMES AS HEADINGS

Especially in qualitative research findings, you may need to find a solution to break down a lengthy findings section. In thesis writing, it is common to witness the findings section divided into multiple chapters in order to help readers' ease of understanding. In many cases, using major themes as headings or subheadings in the findings section could provide a broad overview of the research results.

RESEARCH QUESTIONS AS HEADINGS

Similar to a thematically organized findings section, research questions could serve as headings and subheadings. This is an effective approach, particularly in cases of reporting quantitative and mixed—method research results. This also ensures that each research question/hypothesis is addressed, allowing readers to quickly identify the corresponding answer/result. To organize the results effectively, it may also help to utilize specific themes or key points as subheadings to highlight major findings within each research question.

VIGNETTES

Vignettes are a captivating approach to incorporating narrative contexts and providing a vivid story to draw the readers' attention. Vignettes can serve as a means to introduce themes into your presentation of findings. These vignettes can be strategically placed at the outset of your findings section or within the discussion of each theme. While they typically do not serve as the sole representation of your findings, they can be useful tools to engage the readers and provide a story that illustrates the key findings, themes, and contexts.

USING QUOTATIONS

Using significant or meaningful quotes from participants offers an alternative approach to thematically organizing and presenting research findings. A few approaches are possible to present findings using quotations. One approach is to use the finding itself as a heading and then present an anchoring quote directly after the heading to set the scene before discussing the narrative. Another approach is to use a brief anchoring quote as a heading or subheading to represent the following discussion of the narrative that follows. These quotes will serve as initial evidence, laying the foundation for the description of the following section.

USING EXCERPTS

Similar to using an anchoring quotation, an excerpt from field notes can serve as initial evidence to explain the findings. Similar to using quotations, the finding will be presented as a heading, and the excerpt will be presented immediately after the heading to support the finding. This allows the use of the excerpts as a means to open a discussion about the findings.

Similar to writing a literature review, writing the findings/results section takes multiple iterations and possibly integration of multiple approaches. By involving more than one approach, you can effectively communicate the findings or results of your data analysis. In Kim's (2021) dissertation, vignettes, visuals, quotes, and themes were all utilized to effectively present and discuss major findings from a multiple case study (See Figure 14).

Ways of Reporting to Avoid

As cautioned earlier, there are simply bad ideas when it comes to reporting your findings and results. Here are a few ways of reporting you should watch out for when writing the findings/results section.

Reporting background information of the study: Presenting background information of your research is a job that should have been completed in previous sections. If the results urge the necessity of providing additional background information, it is best to go back to the introduction or other previous sections to revise accordingly.

Ignoring negative results/outcomes: Negative results are possible, such as the results failing to support your initial hypothesis or receiving negative feedback after employing an intervention. This directly leads to ethical conduct of research—you should report the negative results as they are instead of overlooking them. You will have an opportunity to provide further insights and interpretations in the discussion section.

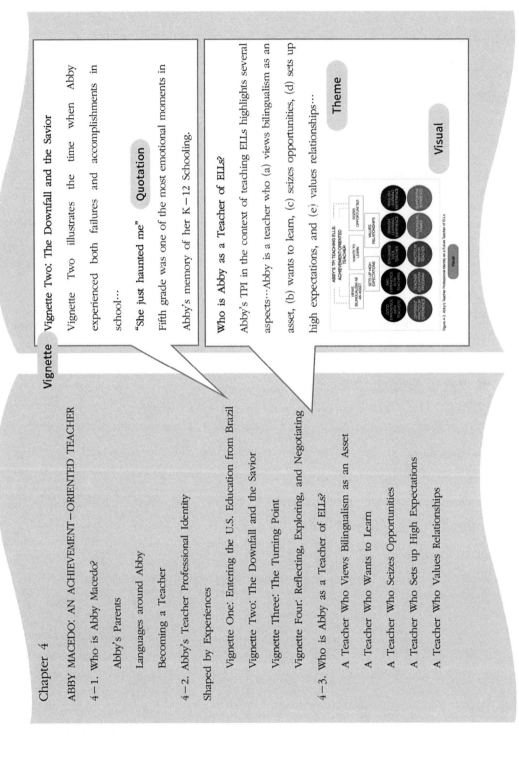

Figure 14. Sample Findings Presentation

Including raw data or intermediate calculations: Unsorted or uncalculated raw data are not typically presented in the findings/results section. Excerpts of interview transcripts or results of data after running tests and calculations are presented in a structured form to support your arguments. If it is necessary to provide raw data or intermediate calculations for any reason, these should be included in the appendices.

Repeating the same data or information: Avoid redundancy of repeating the same data or information that has been presented in the previous section.

Incorrect labeling of data: Make sure you are differentiating figures and tables; and these should be labeled correctly. If there are visual data forms that do not fit into either category, you should consult with someone to provide a correct label.

Providing broader implications of the findings/results: Save highlighting specific implications, recommendations, or significance of the findings for the discussion section. Your thesis is divided into multiple sections for a reason.

Examine sample thesis papers or journal articles within our discipline to understand the conventions regarding structure, content, length, and data visualization, as these may vary across disciplines and even institutions. Novice writers commonly make the mistake of heavily relying on data and quotes instead of providing interpretations of the data. Remember that data are meant to only support your arguments and your research statements. Additionally, carefully consider the order in which your findings/results are presented, leaving room for critical discussions in the following section.

 Writing About··· The Problem

Any and all of the language functions introduced in previous chapters are useful to incorporate in the findings/results section. The linguistic functions that may become more useful in the findings section than others are: Classifying and categorizing and referencing visuals.

CLASSIFYING & CATEGORIZING

Classifying and categorizing is a practice of systematic organization of information into groups or categories based on some shared characteristics, properties, or criteria. The process of classifying and categorizing is something you are expected to do in the data analysis process, which you will then showcase by writing about it in the findings/results section.

- **The** nine **categories of** teacher−self presentations and distributions of respondents **are outlined here.**
  - Dinham, J., Chalk, B., Beltman, S., Glass, C., & Nguyen, B. (2017). Pathways to resilience: how drawings reveal pre−service teachers' core narratives underpinning their future teacher−selves. *Asia−Pacific Journal of Teacher Education, 45*(2), 126−144.

- **Two teachers reported that** they have an intermediate grasp of a foreign language, **while the others** reported an elementary level of foreign language; **two of the 11** had no foreign language competence, although they indicated they took one college−level FL course.
  - Hilliker, S. & Laletina, A. (2018). What do mainstream teachers think, know, and think they know about English language learners? *NYS TESOL Journal, 5*(1), 30−50.

- **Of the** 28 studies, **16 used** mixed research methods, **11 used** qualitative methods, **and one** used quantitative methods. **The learning opportunities studied included** workshops (n=17), summer institutes (n=12), peer collaboration (n=12), coaching or mentoring (n=11), and coursework (n=3).
  - Lucas, T., Strom, K., Bratkovich, M., & Wnuk, J. (2018). Inservice preparation for mainstream teachers of English language learners: A review of the empirical literature. *The Educational Forum, 82*(2), 156−173.

- **From** open-ended survey items completed by bilingual students of color with potential teaching careers, **three prominent themes on** language aligned with themes in our framework: language culture links, diverse linguistic repertoires, and language ideologies.
  - Athanases, S. Z., Banes, L. C., & Wong , J. W. (2015). Diverse language profiles: Leveraging resources of potential bilingual teachers of color. *Bilingual Research Journal, 38* (1), 65−87. doi: 10.1080/15235882.2015.10 17622

REFERENCING VISUALS

Referencing visuals, as stated in the name, involves discussing the visual element in your academic writing. Your findings/results section will likely include tables, charts, figures, or graphs that need explanations or descriptions. Particularly in quantitative research results, it is easy to repeat similar language and sentence structure throughout the findings section. To avoid a dreary reporting of the findings, an inventory of possible language is provided here.

- The common themes emerging from their answers **are included in Table 5**.
  - Cardona Moltó, M. C., Florian, L., Rouse, M. & Stough, L. M. (2010) Attitudes to diversity: a cross-cultural study of education students in Spain, England and the United States, *European Journal of Teacher Education, 33*(3), 245−264, DOI: 10.1080/02619768.2010.495771

- The average scores on feeling of difference across cultural groups showed a general skewedness with mean scores lower than 2 on the Likert scale in almost all dimensions of diversity **(see Table 1)**.
  - Cardona Moltó, M. C., Florian, L., Rouse, M. & Stough, L. M. (2010) Attitudes to diversity: a cross-cultural study of education students in Spain, England and the United States, *European Journal of Teacher Education, 33*(3), 245−264, DOI: 10.1080/02619768.2010.495771

- The McDonald's advertisement **(in Figure 1) features** Hindi/Urdu transliterated in Roman script for localization.
  - Canagarajah, S. & Ashraf, H. (2013).Multilingualism and education in South Asia: Resolving policy/practice dilemmas. *Annual Review of Applied Linguistics, 33*, 258–285.

- **In Figure 2**, the code meshing in a banner that advertises English coaching classes is quite ironic.
  - Canagarajah, S. & Ashraf, H. (2013).Multilingualism and education in South Asia: Resolving policy/practice dilemmas. *Annual Review of Applied Linguistics, 33*, 258–285.

- Again, the summary statistics **are presented in Appendix Table A1.**
  - Shafiq, M. N. & Ross, K. (2010). Educational attainment and attitudes towards war in Muslim countries contemplating war: The cases of Jordan, Lebanon, Pakistan, and Turkey. *Journal of Development Studies, 46*(8), 1424 − 1441.

- **Table 1 illustrates** the position of Finland among some selected nations in Mathematics Olympiads since 1959, when Finland participated for the first time in these games.
  - Sahlberg, P. (2011). PISA in Finland: An education miracle or an obstacle to change?. *CEPS Journal: Center for Educational Policy Studies Journal, 1*(3), 119.

- **Table 2 shows** participation of Finland in major international student assessment studies since early 1960s, when the First International Mathematics Study was launched (Sahlberg, 2011).
  - Sahlberg, P. (2011). PISA in Finland: An education miracle or an obstacle to change?. *CEPS Journal: Center for Educational Policy Studies Journal, 1*(3), 119.

- In science, the main focus of the PISA 2006 survey, Finnish students outperformed their peers in all 56 countries, **some of which are shown in Figure 1.**
  - Sahlberg, P. (2011). PISA in Finland: An education miracle or an obstacle to change?. *CEPS Journal: Center for Educational Policy Studies Journal, 1*(3), 119.

- Finland, as one of the strong performers in PISA, has the most even educational performance profile of all OECD countries, with only about 7.7% of national reading literacy variation from between−school variance, the OECD variance being 42% (OECD, 2010a). This means that the affect of pupils' family background, especially their socioeconomic status, in academic achievement is smaller in countries that also have a higher overall national achievement score, **as shown in Figure 4.**
  - Sahlberg, P. (2011). PISA in Finland: An education miracle or an obstacle to change?. *CEPS Journal: Center for Educational Policy Studies Journal, 1*(3), 119.

Reflection Questions

▸ What are the key findings of your data analysis results?

▸ What presentation method do you plan to incorporate in writing your findings/results section?

▸ How would you organize your findings/results section? Draft an outline of your findings/results section using headings and subheadings.

Wrapping up
: Writing Discussion and Conclusion

Opening Questions

- What information should be included in a discussion and conclusion section?
- Why do people say that writing the discussion requires extended experience and skills?

In this chapter, you will···

- Identify key points to include in a discussion/conclusion section.
- Develop an outline of a discussion section for your thesis writing.

As you wrap up your research and thesis writing, you should start considering the implications and suggestions that arise from your research. The discussion section is a challenging part for novice writers and researchers. After providing your interpretation of the findings, you need to carry those interpretations further to the next level and carefully contemplate what those interpretations mean in a broader context. Deriving from your findings, you should take the time to reinterpret existing theories or teaching practices. Allocate ample time to reflect and articulate the discussion and conclusion section.

The Role of a Discussion Section

The most crucial component of your thesis is commonly known as the discussion section. Even in scholarly articles published in journals, the discussion section is often the first (or sometimes the only) section readers pay attention to in order to get a quick but in−depth understanding of your research. The discussion section involves illuminating and interpreting your results within the theoretical or conceptual framework as well as your research aims, questions, and purposes. You should examine the implications of the findings/results, acknowledge the limitations (if it is a quantitative or mixed−method research), and provide recommendations. Through this process, you are naturally constructing an argument to strengthen your conclusion. Commonly, a discussion section includes the following elements, which are sometimes divided into separate sub−sections and headings.

- A summary of the key findings/results
- Answers to the research questions
- Interpretation of the findings/results
- Implications of the findings/results
- The limitations of the findings/results
- Suggestions or practical applications of the findings/results
- Recommendations for further investigations
- Concluding remarks

One of the distinguishing characteristics between quantitative and qualitative research designs is the length of a discussion section. While qualitative research often demands a lengthy findings section due to the lengthy data and the primary focus on the researcher's interpretation of the data, quantitative research demands a rather lengthy discussion section to provide further interpretations of the data presented in the results section. Oftentimes, the content in the discussion section overlaps with that of the conclusion section, which is why the two sections are combined in some cases. Sometimes, there are institutions or journals that require including a separate conclusion section. This is simply a matter of formatting that you might need to check before writing your research thesis or article.

Steps for Composing a Discussion Section

A common pitfall for novice writers and researchers is summarizing findings in the discussion section without progressing to the next appropriate step. Limit your summary to a concise paragraph and avoid extended summaries. Follow these steps to compose the discussion section effectively.

Step 1. Provide key findings and insights: Articulate the major or key findings derived from your research. On the one hand, this involves summarizing your research findings. On the other hand, this requires concise summarizing and highlighting that you would like to incorporate in the discussion section. Practice this by asking yourself what the one or two most important findings might be in your research.

Step 2. Elaborate: Break down these key findings or insights into several bullet points. Explain the significance, meaning, and various aspects associated with each bullet point.

Step 3. Establish connections: Draw connections between these bullet points and specific research findings and results. Also, establish connections between your insights and existing research findings, recognizing that, while your research is novel, certain aspects may align with findings from prior research.

Step 4. Emphasize the originality of your research: Highlight the distinctive nature of your research findings/results. While previous research may have addressed some aspects, underscore the new and unique contributions your research brings to the table.

Step 5. Address the "so what?" question: Deliberate on and answer the "so what?" question. This is easier said than done in reality. As you put together your discussion section, engage in a mental practice of constantly asking yourself, "So what?". Having presented the key takeaway, so what? What is the significance? Why should fellow researchers and/or practitioners take note of this research and its conclusion? What is its meaning, value, and impact?

Figure 15 provides a sample illustration of the mind mapping process of constructing a discussion section in Kim's (2021) dissertation.

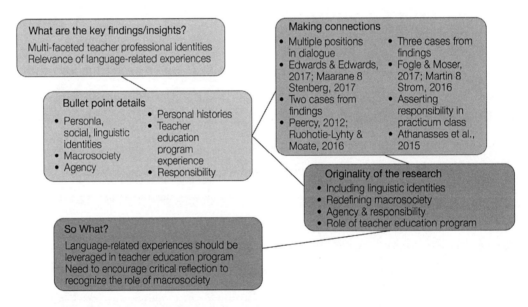

Figure 15. Sample Mind Mapping Process of Constructing Discussion

Like any other section, your discussion section requires time and an iterative cycle of writing and rewriting. It is also important to continue asking yourself the "so what?" question over and over again until you reach a point where there is no way to answer it.

Guiding Questions for the Discussion

The following questions might help you to construct some discussion points and interpretive statements.

- What do the key findings or insights mean to educators or students? What do they mean to the field of research?
- How do other studies support my findings?
- How do your findings contribute to the existing body of knowledge?
- How do your findings address the gaps in previous research?
- How do your findings diverge from other studies?
- What are the practical applications of my research? How can teachers, educators, or policymakers utilize the findings of your research?
- How can your findings contribute to developing educational programs and curricula?
- How do your findings inform the understanding of educational achievements and outcomes?
- How do your findings carry value to all stakeholders in the field of education?
- What areas of research may still need exploration, and how does your research contribute to that recognition?
- Do your findings challenge or support existing theories or concepts? In what way?
- How does your research inform our current understanding of methodological approaches in educational research?
- How does your research contribute to the body of knowledge in the field of education?
- How should future research address the questions that remain unanswered or underexplored in your study?
- What is some future work you might suggest considering the limitations of your research?

Remember that the discussion section is where you claim the meaning, importance, and relevance of your findings and your entire research project. You should be knowledgeable of the findings and the literature review you provided in the previous sections and make intentional connections to make claims and arguments supported by the contents in the two sections.

Common Mistakes and Pitfalls in a Discussion

There are a few common mistakes and pitfalls made by novice writers or emerging scholars. Here, we introduce some common mistakes you should be aware of when you are writing your discussion. However, keep in mind that a discussion section is a challenging section, even for experienced writers and researchers.

Repeating findings/results: Although a summary of your findings and results may be included in your discussion section, as cautioned earlier, the summary should not overpower the discussion section. Novice writers also attempt to recycle statements made in the findings/results section. You may need to refer to your findings and results in order to support the claims you make in the discussion section, but your discussion section should not be wasted with a repetition of statements you have already made.

Introducing new results: As you construct your discussion section, you may encounter a moment when you realize a very important piece of finding or result you cannot draw on to support your claim because it was not included in the findings/results section. In this case, you need to go back and revise the previous section because the discussion section is not the place to introduce any new results.

Overstatements: Feeling the pressure to make significant contributions and with an attempt to answer the "so what?" question, novice writers and researchers may fall into the trap of inflating their claims. Avoid making these overstatements or overinterpretations that you cannot support with your findings and results.

Understatements: Another common mistake made by novice writers and researchers is underselling their research. Your research is not perfect, and nobody expects it to have any flaws. This does not mean you need to undermine your research by putting too much emphasis on its limitations or the research question that was not fully explored. You may need to discuss the limitations, but only as a means to strengthen the credibility of your research.

Statements unrelated to the research questions or aims: You may encounter parts of the data that reveal unexpected findings—results or findings you did not aim to examine. You might mention them as a recommendation for future research, but these are not the main focus of your discussion section. Your discussion is dedicated to providing the implications and interpretations of your research findings based on the initial research questions and aims you proposed.

Concluding your Research and Thesis Writing

The conclusion is not always a separate section in the research and thesis writing piece. Having a separate limitation and/or conclusion section depends on your research design, the volume of your findings/results, the depth of your discussions, and departmental or institutional guidelines. In the case of graduate students, it may simply depend on your committee chair or advisor's preference. In any case, it cannot be harmful to know how to conclude your research and thesis writing. The following are a few tips for writing the conclusion section:

Provide key points and insights: The key here is to provide very succinct statements to summarize your research. Why should anyone bother reading your thesis? If you had to sum up your answer in one sentence, what would it be?

Address the limitations (if any): The limitations are often important to address in quantitative or mixed−method design research. In qualitative research, some unexpected insights or shortcomings in answering the research question may be included as well. Try to balance this with the key achievements/outcomes of your research.

Provide recommendations: The conclusion section is a suitable place to provide recommendations for future research and practice. Your research could have made contributions to inform theoretical foundations, research methodologies, or practices in education. The findings also could have shed light on areas that need further exploration in the future. These are all good recommendations to make in the conclusion.

An effective conclusion reiterates the key aspects of your thesis and clarifies to the readers why your research is significant, applicable, and relevant. It is typically briefer than other sections of your thesis and aims to provide recommendations for readers and fellow researchers. Along with the discussion section, it is one of the sections readers pay more attention to than others.

 Writing About··· Discussion and Conclusion

While all language functions are useful everywhere, two particular language functions may be deemed more useful in the last section of your thesis: making recommendations and stating limitations.

MAKING RECOMMENDATIONS

Making recommendations means offering informed suggestions, such as suggestions informed by the findings and results of your research. This may involve providing practice steps to address certain issues or to improve situations.

- **Perhaps the most important finding emerging from this review is that,** to be linguistically responsive to ELLs, mainstream teachers need some knowledge of second language development—knowledge that provides a foundation for understanding ELLs and designing instruction for them.
  - Villegas, A. M., SaizdeLaMora, K., Martin, A. D., & Mills, T. (2018). Preparing future mainstream teachers to teach English language learners: A review of the empirical literature. *The Educational Forum, 82*(2), 138−155.

- **This finding suggests that** there is a need to advance a broader concept of culture, one that would transcend traditions, customs, and rituals and encompass language, communication, ideology, and cultural mindset beyond the traditional setting of foreign language studies and TESOL.

- Hilliker, S. & Laletina, A. (2018). What do mainstream teachers think, know, and think they know about English language learners? *NYS TESOL Journal, 5*(1), 30−50.

• In the TESOL-TE **field, more empirical research is needed to examine how** teachers learn to educate ELLs, how teacher educators contingently support teacher learning in the moment, and how teachers integrate effective instruction for multilingual students in schools where these types of practices are not the norm.

- Daniel, S. M. & Pray, L. (2017). Learning to teach English language learners: A study of elementary school teachers' sense−making in an ELL endorsement program. *TESOL Quarterly, 51*(4), 787−819.

• As Pierre Bourdieu reminds us, **one of the most important activities scholars can engage in** during this time of economic rationalism and imperial neo−conservatism **is to** analyse critically the production and circulation of these discourses and their effects on the lives of so many people in so many nations (Bourdieu, 1998, p. 29). **I would urge us to** take this role even more seriously than we have in the past.

- Apple, M. (2001). Comparing neo−liberal projects and inequality in education. *Comparative Education, 37*(4), 409−423.

• **Further quantitative and qualitative research on** educational institutions and curricula in the four countries **can provide details on** how educational attainment can promote peaceful conflict resolution.

- Shafiq, M. N. & Ross, K. (2010). Educational attainment and attitudes towards war in Muslim countries contemplating war: The cases of Jordan, Lebanon, Pakistan, and Turkey. *Journal of Development Studies, 46*(8), 1424−1441

- Finally, **we encourage research on** the robustness of our findings using alternative data sources. Currently, there are several surveys underway at collecting public opinion data in the Muslim world, such as The Arab Barometer and The Asian Barometer (both collected by an international consortium of universities and research centres) and the Poll of the Muslim World (collected by Gallup). Since these surveys contain slightly different questions on attitudes towards international conflict, **there are opportunities to gain a more complete understanding** between the educational attainment and attitudes towards war in Jordan, Lebanon, Pakistan, and Turkey.
  - Shafiq, M. N. & Ross, K. (2010). Educational attainment and attitudes towards war in Muslim countries contemplating war: The cases of Jordan, Lebanon, Pakistan, and Turkey. *Journal of Development Studies*, *46*(8), 1424−1441

- **It is important that** international student assessment studies **are used wisely** in policy making and education reform architecture. There is much more information in these existing studies that governments and the media have been able to use for better policies and deeper news reporting. Before considering any new forms of data collection, **we should make better use of what we already have.** PISA and other international benchmark tools **are important for** any government that cares about education in an open, globalised world. **Using** these data for the good of our teachers and students **is a continuing challenge for us all.**
  - Sahlberg, P. (2011). PISA in Finland: An education miracle or an obstacle to change?. *CEPS Journal: Center for Educational Policy Studies Journal*, *1*(3), 119.

- Having said this, however, **we need to be cautious not to ignore** historical specificities and comparative realities. Social movements, existing ideological formations, and institutions in civil society and the state **may provide** some support for countervailing logics. In some cases, in those nations with stronger and more extensive histories of social democratic policies and visions of collective positive freedoms, the neo−liberal emphasis on the market has been significantly mediated.

- Apple, M. (2001). Comparing neo−liberal projects and inequality in education. *Comparative Education, 37*(4), 409−423.

- **More research is necessary,** however, in order to understand how attending schools, colleges, and universities during periods of violent conflict, as opposed to periods of relative calm, might affect students' attitudes.
  - Shafiq, M. N. & Ross, K. (2010). Educational attainment and attitudes towards war in Muslim countries contemplating war: The cases of Jordan, Lebanon, Pakistan, and Turkey. *Journal of Development Studies, 46*(8), 1424−1441

- **This essay has argued that** providing refugees with a platform to tell their stories **can help move the public conversation surrounding** immigration beyond the frame of illegality in which immigrants and refugees are often confined. **It has also suggested that** new interdisciplinary models in the academy **might be necessary** as we continue to fight for the rights and dignity of migrants and refugees mindful of the quintessential immigrant rights dictum that "no human being is illegal."
  - Pulitano, E. (2013). In liberty's shadow: the discourse of refugees and asylum seekers in critical race theory and immigration law/politics. *Identities, 20*(2), 172−189.

- **There is, however, a need for more detailed studies that** experiment with translanguaging in a variety of content and language classrooms to assess its effectiveness on ways of knowing and making sense of the world.
  - Makalela, L. (2015). Translanguaging as a vehicle for epistemic access: Cases for reading comprehension and multilingual interactions. *Per Linguam: a Journal of Language Learning=Per Linguam: Tydskrif vir*

Taalaanleer, 31(1), 15 − 29.

STATING LIMITATIONS

Stating limitations pertains to an explicit acknowledgment of identified constraints, shortcomings, or boundaries of your study. As mentioned earlier, stating limitations in a quantitative or mixed−methods research design is critical to the credibility of the research. Typically, aspects that may impact the validity, generalizability, or scope of the findings are addressed. In qualitative studies, there might be space to state the limitations of certain studies, theories, or methodologies in the discussion section.

- **While these results show** important developments in language pedagogy, **they should be interpreted in the light of the study's inherent limitations of being a reflective enquiry relying on a small sample.** However, these results provide scope for further research in similar contexts of preparing pre−service teachers through a translanguaging approach.
  - Makalela, L. (2015). Moving out of linguistic boxes: The effects of translanguaging strategies for multilingual classrooms. *Language and education, 29*(3), 200 − 217.

- **PISA also suffers some limitations:** It assesses a very limited amount of what is taught in schools; **it can adopt only a** cross−sectional design; **it ignores the role and contribution of teachers; and the way its results are presented** —in some, at least, of its tables – **encourages a superficial, 'league table'** reading of what should be a more interesting but essentially more complex picture. (Mortimore, 2009, p. 2)
  - Sahlberg, P. (2011). PISA in Finland: An education miracle or an obstacle to change?. *CEPS Journal: Center for Educational Policy Studies Journal, 1*(3), 119.

- Thus, **it is critical to understand** how neuroscience may support good educational practices while at the same time temper the excitement **with an** understanding of the limitations of neuroscience applications to special education.

- Alferink, L. A., & Farmer−Dougan, V. (2010). Brain−(not) based education: Dangers of misunderstanding and misapplication of neuroscience research. *Exceptionality, 18*(1), 42−52.

- **Two limitations of this study were** the quasi−experimental design and voluntary participation of treatment teachers.
  - Short, D. J., Fidelman, C. G., & Louguit, M. (2012). Developing academic language in English language learners through sheltered instruction. *Tesol Quarterly, 46*(2), 334−361.

- **The limitations of the** perspectival dualist framework **surface when we** introduce viewpoints that challenge the "social preconditions of individual autonomy" as given (Honneth, 2003, p. 179). In other words, when we question the social processes that lead to individual autonomy, competing conceptualizations of individual and group difference emerge. Furthermore, when, as in Fraser's framework, social movements are used **as the sole indicator of** "moral discontent in developed societies," **we tend to neglect** everyday microlevel social processes that have not yet been publicly articulated but still contribute to "social misery and moral injustice" (Honneth, 2003, pp. 113−115).
  - North, C. E. (2006). More than words? Delving into the substantive meaning (s) of "social justice" in education. *Review of Educational Research, 76*(4), 507−535.

- Although exploratory, **the present study is not without limitations. First, the sample size** for some cultural groups **was small. Second, issues related to** cultural equivalence and/or cultural bias **were not addressed directly. As with any study of** attitudes, investigations of the construct are mediated by the specific measures used. Thus, the cross−cultural variation obtained **may** be due to a lack of cultural equivalence and/or cultural bias in the measures used or a lack of reliability or validity in the measures used. **Third, the sampling strategy**, in this case convenience samples, **places limits on the** conclusions and generalisations about national variations in attitudes and beliefs toward difference. **There is a need for subsequent studies to** incorporate a follow–up strategy that would allow more qualitative explanations of each domain. […] The etic and emic properties also **need to be validated on a larger sample** and through a **more robust statistical procedure** (e.g., structural equation modelling). **And finally, it is necessary to consider the extent to which** the respondents perceived that there were 'right' and 'wrong' answers to these questions.

- Cardona Moltó, M. C., Florian, L., Rouse, M. & Stough, L. M. (2010) Attitudes to diversity: a cross-cultural study of education students in Spain, England and the United States, *European Journal of Teacher Education, 33*(3), 245–264, DOI: 10.1080/02619768.2010.495771

- Krashen's input hypothesis may be 'a bucket full of holes' as Ellis (1990: 106) asserts, but comprehensible input is certainly the most important single factor (to the exclusion of much else) – in immersion settings. Swan, who talked of the '3hpw learners' (three hours per week), asserts that the naturalistic communication–driven approach so much in vogue today **has serious limitations,** 'especially as regards the systematic teaching of new linguistic material.

  - Butzkamm, W. (2011). Why make them crawl if they can walk? Teaching with mother tongue support. *RELC Journal, 42*(3), 379–391.

Reflection Questions

▸ What are the key elements/contents you need to include in a discussion and conclusion section?

▸ Create an outline of the information you plan to include in your discussion/conclusion section. Ask yourself the "so what?" question until you run out of answers. How difficult or easy was the process? Why?

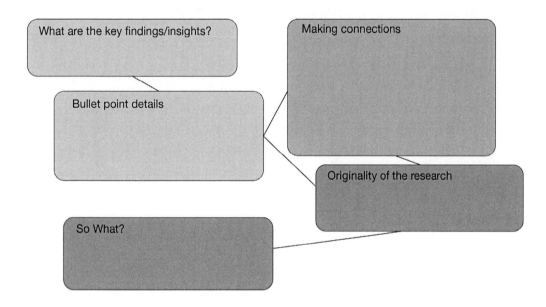

PART

III

Furthering Research
and Academic Writing

14

Self-checklist for Academic Writing and Research

Opening Questions

- What are some key takeaways for you after learning about research and thesis writing?
- How does developing academic writing skills contribute to developing research skills?

In this chapter, you will···

- Interpret the cyclical nature of academic writing and research skills.
- Review and evaluate your research and academic writing progress.

Academic writing and research are inseparable. They are both a part of a process in your personal and professional development as well as your scholarly pursuit.

Cycle of Academic Writing and Research Processes

As much as writing your thesis is an iterative process, developing your research skills is embedded in the cycle of academic writing processes (see Figure 16). The steps and procedures you take in academic writing are a direct reflection of your ethical and rigorous conduct of research. In the cycle of identifying the problem, gathering information, creating your aim, and drafting, academic writing and research take the same iterative process. More importantly, one complements another, which means advancing your academic writing as much as developing your research skills helps improve the other. By improving your academic writing skills, you are honing your skills to generate precise research ideas. As you craft your research skills, your academic writing skills also advance to articulate complex concepts in a more understandable manner.

Figure 16. Cycle of Academic Writing and Research Processes

Self-checklist for Research and Academic Writing

As you progress through your research and thesis writing, it is always helpful to have a handy checklist to monitor, review, and evaluate your progress. The following self−checklist could serve as a tool to ensure you are staying on track in your research and thesis writing. This may also be useful in planning and executing any research projects followed by an academic writing task.

<u>Self−checklist for Research & Academic Writing</u>
Check off the box if you have···
☐ Identified a problem through a problem−solving approach.
☐ Surveyed relevant literature concerning the problem.
☐ Identified the gap in the literature.
☐ Established a clear and narrowed−down problem statement.
☐ Searched and collected related literature.
☐ Identified similar studies and the gap in the literature.
☐ Drafted a summary of previous research.
☐ Established research question(s).
☐ Searched and read literature to establish the theoretical/conceptual framework.
☐ Organized the literature review based on the research aim and theoretical foundation.
☐ Revised research purpose, question(s), and theoretical foundation.
☐ Established a methodology that aligns with research philosophies.
☐ Developed research tools, data collection, and analysis methods.
☐ Submitted and received an IRB review approval (if applicable).
☐ Began collecting data according to the data collection plan.
☐ Began analyzing data according to the data analysis plan.
☐ Reflected on and evaluated data analysis findings/results.
☐ Developed and organized the best way to present the findings/results.
☐ Reviewed and revised the findings/results.

☐ Took the proper steps to make claims and interpretations for the discussion.

☐ Established the takeaway and originality of the research.

☐ Answered the "so what?" question.

☐ Reviewed and revised the discussion/conclusion.

☐ Reviewed and revised the abstract and introduction.

☐ Reviewed and proofread the entire thesis/writing piece.

Self–evaluation allows you to reflect on and evaluate your own work as you take each step of the writing process. This helps you to identify your strengths and weaknesses as a writer and researcher. Furthermore, a regular self–assessment pinpoints specific tasks or areas that need improvement, therefore enhancing your research and writing skills. The above self–checklist, which provides items in a rather chronological order, also helps you to be aware of the next steps and contributes to setting goals as you continue the journey of academic writing and research. Keep in mind that, ultimately, the most important task in academic writing and research is constant review, reflection, and revision. This will move you forward and facilitate your growth as you progress.

Reflection Questions

▸ What do you find as your strengths and weaknesses in academic writing or research? How can developing academic writing and research skills grow as a researcher and writer?

▸ Utilize the self—checklist to evaluate your writing and research progress. What are some steps you end up missing, and why do you think that is?

Dissemination Beyond the Thesis

- What does dissemination of research mean?
- Why is it important to think about the dissemination of your research?
- How many dissemination channels or methods can you think of?

  In this chapter, you will···

- Recognize the importance of disseminating your research.
- Compare different dissemination channels available for you to share your knowledge and research.

Keep in mind that once you complete your thesis and research, your scholarly journey has just begun. Whether you take a path seeking industry jobs or academic jobs, it is your responsibility as a researcher to find a proper channel to disseminate your research.

Dissemination of Research: What Does it Mean?

Before we provide ways to properly disseminate your research beyond the thesis, it is important to tackle what it means to disseminate your research and the value it carries. When we discuss dissemination of research, we are referring to the sharing and communication of your research results and findings with a broader audience in the academic and public community. This also involves the process of making your research accessible to those who were not intimately involved in the research planning and execution process. Thus, a rather skillful set of writing and communication abilities is required in order to effectively deliver your research insights and findings to people who may not know you, your research area, or your communication styles. By disseminating your research, the purpose is to contribute to the body of knowledge and practice in your field, inspire discussions, and provide opportunities for others to build upon your research findings.

Below are a few reasons why the act of disseminating knowledge is important for an emerging scholar:

- *Knowledge contribution:* By disseminating knowledge, you can contribute to the collective knowledge in your field. This allows the research community to further your knowledge and findings, contributing to the overall advancement of knowledge.

- *Constructing scholarly identities:* It is hard to see yourself as a researcher and scholar immediately after completing your thesis research. You have made the first step into the scholarly community by completing your thesis research. Disseminating your research helps construct your scholarly identity as a researcher by publishing in academic journals or presenting at scholarly conferences. You are beginning to let your name be known by people in the academic community, providing you with an identity marker as a scholar and researcher.

- *Feedback and dialogues*: Dissemination of your research in a broader scholarly community also allows you an opportunity to receive constructive feedback from peer reviewers and fellow researchers who are as committed to the field as you are. Furthermore, the process of disseminating your research and receiving feedback engages you in dialogues and communications with those involved in the field.

- *Opportunities for impact and application*: There is no doubt that dissemination of your research helps make an impact on the research and teaching communities. By sharing your research with a broader audience, you are informing the research and teaching communities to advance the theories, methodologies, and practice. Your research may allow further applications in research and teaching, which will make an impact on the field of education.

- *Personal and professional development*: Needless to say, dissemination of your research will contribute to your personal and professional development. As mentioned in Chapter 1, academic writing skills alone contribute to your personal and professional development. Aligned with the point we made about academic writing and research skills enriching your capabilities (see Chapter 14), disseminating your research develops some essential transferrable skills, such as communication skills, critical thinking, and reflective thinking skills.

Dissemination Channels Beyond the Thesis

There are many available options for you to disseminate your research beyond the thesis you wrote. Here, we introduce several dissemination channels but keep in mind that there are more channels as information technology enables limitless capabilities.

- *Publication through academic journals*: This is the most common dissemination channel for many academics. Particularly, if you are trying to pursue a career path in academia or research−oriented careers, publishing through reputable peer−reviewed academic journals is considered almost a requirement. Whether you are choosing to publish out of obligation or to boost your scholarly identity, a publication through academic journals allows you to disseminate your research further within the academic community.

- *Publication through practitioner journals*: Depending on your research topic, other practitioner−oriented journals are a viable option to consider. This allows you to make a direct impact on the teaching and learning community where your research could be applied to a school or classroom. Especially if your research involves developing a curriculum, program, or teaching practices, a practitioner journal could make a larger and more immediate impact compared to academic journals, which often have limited access for practitioners.

- *Conference presentations*: Conference presentations can be a less stressful and easier first step to disseminate your research. The peer−review process can be less restrictive, and tailoring your research may require less preparation and time, as the time allocated for you to share your research might be 15 minutes to 45 minutes. You also get an opportunity to receive rather immediate feedback from those who attend your session, which can inform you to make the appropriate changes and improvements for the next publishing of your work.

- *Publishing a book*: Depending on your discipline and career path, a book publication might be an option you need to consider. Also, the type of research, such as longitudinal research or large−scale research, may determine the necessity of disseminating your research through a book publication. Some authors jump into the book publication process with the expectation that little tailoring will be involved since their thesis is long, and inevitably, books are long, too. Unlike journal article publication, it seems reasonable to expect little tailoring, trimming, and rewriting. However, your thesis is a piece of written work that preserves its originality and copyright in its entirety. If you are familiar with the term self−plagiarism, publishing your own thesis in a book form without making any substantial changes will fall under committing self−plagiarism. That means you need to rewrite everything in order to publish your research as a book. However, once you complete the work and publish a book about your research, the impact you can have on the public audience is more than any other dissemination channel.

- *Blogging and other social media*: Blogging, social media, or other digital communication channels, such as writing an article in a newsletter or other periodicals, is another option to reach a broader audience. This is also considered a low−stakes and less−stressful opportunity to disseminate your research without undergoing a rigorous and oftentimes harsh peer−review process. This also allows you to reach a more general audience who may benefit from your research and immediately apply it in the field. Another benefit is developing writing and communication skills to discuss your research with the public—those who are not used to the academic language and jargon you use.

- *Collaboration and networking*: Collaboration and networking opportunities are everywhere to help you disseminate your research further. Commonly, the abovementioned dissemination channels lead to collaboration and networking opportunities, which allow you to share your knowledge and research with colleagues, researchers, and scholars who have similar interests. Building connections through collaboration and networking will also ultimately benefit you in establishing your scholarly identity and reputation.

Rewriting your thesis and tailoring your writing piece to a specific dissemination channel is as much a challenging task as writing and completing the thesis. However, remember it is the first step you take as a professional and academic writer and scholar. Driven by your passion for research and the advancement of your field, you should actively seek opportunities to disseminate your research and spread your knowledge throughout the global academic and public community.

Reflection Questions

▸ Compare the various dissemination channels outlined in this chapter. What is the dissemination channel you would like to try out? What are the advantages and disadvantages of the dissemination channel you chose?

▸ What kind of impact would you like to make ultimately as a scholar and researcher? Why?

Lifelong Development of Skills

- What does it mean to be a lifelong learner?
- What are some skills you have developed throughout your life up until now?

In this chapter, you will…

- Illustrate your plans and future career paths to expand upon your research.
- Examine the skills you have acquired as a result of developing academic writing and research skills.

In this chapter, we would like to return to the points we made about academic writing skills and their contribution to your personal and professional development (see Chapter 1). Honing your academic writing skills, interwoven with the development of research and thesis writing tasks, develops you holistically in various aspects. Your awareness of the skills you developed places you on the journey of skills development as a lifelong learner, researcher, scholar, and educator.

Reflecting on Your Journey

The term and activity, reflection, is used commonly and frequently throughout this book and possibly throughout your journey in academic writing. Reflecting is an important skill but also a great tool to strive for lifelong development, growth, and learning.

The following questions could be helpful to think back on your journey thus far and establish concrete plans for moving forward.

- What are the lessons you learned from taking graduate−level courses?
- What new insights did you gain regarding the local teaching and education communities? How do they inform your research endeavors?
- How did the exposure to scholarly research and communities motivate or inspire you?
- How did you learn to cope with stressful and challenging moments?
- How did the exposure and familiarity of literature written in English inform you as a writer and scholar?
- What cultural norms and practices did you notice from engaging in academic communication and interaction?
- What are the hidden cultural norms and practices in the academic community that need to be more explicit?
- What lessons did you learn through the academic writing and research process?
- What advice would you give to emerging scholars and writers in your field?
- How did your understanding of the field of education and related societal

problems change over time?

- What are some educational and societal problems that still need to be addressed and explored?
- What are some skills or knowledge you feel like you still need to develop for your own personal and professional growth?

An active engagement in self−reflection not only helps you to be more self−aware but also encourages you to be more growth− and improvement−oriented as you encounter challenges and obstacles. Let these questions facilitate your lifelong development as a person and a scholar. Some people may say that earning a graduate or terminal degree is the destination of graduate studies. We believe that you are simply at the starting point of your long academic and professional journey.

Expansion and Development of Expertise and Skills

We would like to engage in a discussion on how to expand and develop your expertise and skills at the starting point of your academic journey. How can you best leverage your experience, knowledge, and training, regardless of the career path you take for your future?

EXPANDING YOUR EXPERTISE

Upon obtaining your graduate or terminal degree, various research avenues, as well as career opportunities are available for you. While it is common, especially in the STEM (Science, Technology, Engineering, and Mathematics) field, to pursue an industry career after completing a graduate program, the humanities and social science fields may look like there are limited paths to choose from after obtaining a higher degree. It should be noted that any field of study, regardless of the discipline, is adapting to the changing society. This means there are so many possibilities for you to expand your expertise.

In the case of choosing an academic career path, people commonly believe that they need to concentrate on the specific area they chose as their thesis research topic. For instance, Kim's dissertation research focused on language teacher identity construction in teacher education programs, while Lee's dissertation research focused on language teacher self−efficacy in teacher education programs. As much as these were valuable research projects, both researchers recognized the need to expand our expertise due to several societal changes and issues. The teacher education field is shrinking as we speak due to low birth rates and the depreciation of the teaching profession. This means there are fewer students enrolled in teacher education programs and a stark decrease in college student enrollment in general. Furthermore, the advent of educational technology opened more needs for research incorporating technology in education. Thus, both authors pursued opportunities to expand their knowledge, research areas, and expertise.

In the case of pursuing other career paths outside of academia, we observed numerous opportunities available. Many of our colleagues chose a path to stay close to the practitioners by teaching in schools or supervising school teachers, such as developing professional development programs. Others choose a path in higher education, oftentimes searching for ways to advance their education at the postsecondary level while maintaining educational principles applied to K−12 education. Again, the sky is the limit, and there are numerous paths to pursue regardless of your specialization and concentration in your graduate studies. This commonly requires you to take a look at the transferrable skills you developed and "sell" those skills to your future employers.

DEVELOPMENT OF TRANSFERRABLE SKILLS

As you develop your academic writing and research skills, you are simultaneously acquiring a multitude of transferrable skills. Knowing which skills constitute transferrable skills and recognizing specific transferrable skills commonly desired by employers may make it easier for you to boost your resume or CV (curriculum Vitae) and become a desirable candidate.

Some of the skills you may cultivate during your journey as a novice academic writer and emerging scholar include:

- Project management

- Data organization and management
- Supervision and coaching
- Communication
- Metalinguistic awareness
- Leadership
- Team building

Project coordination

- Creative problem−solving
- Inductive and deductive reasoning
- Administrative
- Proficiency in learning management systems
- Public speaking and presentation
- Consulting and advising
- Interviewing
- Multitasking
- Time management
- Graphic design

The following are some of the many transferrable skills commonly desired by employers. You may notice a lot of overlap between the two lists.

- Problem−solving
- Analytical reasoning
- Critical thinking
- Leadership
- Adaptability
- Teamwork
- Written communication
- Verbal communication
- Confidence
- Nonverbal communication
- Responsiveness

- Active listening
- Creativity
- Attention to detail
- Organization
- Relationship building
- Computer skills
- Management
- Collaboration
- Self—awareness
- Conflict resolution
- Time management
- Patience
- Interpersonal skills
- Goal setting
- Decision—making
- Empathy
- Evaluation skills
- Self—motivation
- Technology literacy
- Process improvement

Although not listed in the first list, you might have noticed there are some skills you indeed developed throughout your journey as you were pursuing your research and academic endeavors. It is beneficial to recognize how your time spent conducting research and writing your thesis shaped your development in transferrable skills. Keeping track of the skills you developed during this period allows you to highlight your potential and capabilities on your resume, turning your graduate studies into a rich asset beyond a simple degree.

Reflection Questions

▶ Think about how you would leverage your experience and knowledge moving forward. What career paths are you considering? How could you expand upon your academic writing and research experiences?

▶ What transferrable skills have you acquired during the time of obtaining your graduate degree? What are some transferrable skills you would still like to develop further?

Concluding Remarks

As we conclude, we would like to provide our anecdotes and how we envision this book making an impact. We observed some graduate students rushing to obtain their diplomas quickly while neglecting the importance of producing high−quality research and writing. This is at the expense of the quality of their research and learning opportunities to grow personally and professionally. It is not uncommon for graduate students or emerging scholars to feel extreme pressure to show results as soon as possible. This may sometimes result in taking shortcuts and cutting corners. When we were in graduate school struggling to complete our dissertation writing, we often heard the advice, "A good dissertation is a done dissertation." Obviously, there is a point where you must admit to the imperfections inherent in the early stages of your academic journey. However, it is noteworthy to also keep in mind that the road to reaching a "done dissertation" is and should be accompanied by the principles of academic rigor and dedication. Our own experiences during the challenging journey of completing our dissertations exposed us to the temptations of choosing fast results over a rigorous process. We have seen and heard those who advocate for swift completion, emphasizing "getting it done." Yet, we want to stress the importance of balancing this urgency with a commitment to scholarly excellence. With each step of your research and academic writing, cultivate curiosity and a problem−solving mindset. This will not only enrich your professional and personal experiences but will also contribute to developing transferable skills you can apply throughout your life. Conducting original and impactful research is undeniably demanding, marked by setbacks and feedback that may, at times, seem overly harsh. You will develop some attachment to your research and writing pieces. This makes it even more challenging to change the course of action or the direction, which is also inevitable in research and academic writing. Keep in mind that enduring difficult times and overcoming obstacles is the crucible in which you will develop problem—solving, critical thinking, and analytical skills unlike anyone else. It is through this rigorous process of investigating, exploring, and problem—solving that you will distinguish yourself and make a lasting difference.

By writing this book, we hoped to provide a platform for reflection on your journey of academic and professional growth. We encourage you to be thoughtful at every step and consider some of the guiding principles we highlighted in this book. By being intentional, as we recommended in these chapters, you will develop a profound appreciation for engaging in scholarly endeavors. Your journey of learning and developing academic writing and research skills could be transformational to cultivating yourself as an independent researcher, a global scholar, and a leader. Embrace the learning process, and let the development of academic writing and research skills be the bedrock of your personal and professional achievements.

Our aspiration is to move beyond the surface—level understanding of research and thesis writing to move forward to understanding the true value and joy of engaging in research. Our sincere hope is that all emerging scholars in the field of education will strive for high—quality research and academic writing as the two pillars supporting their aspirations and contributing to the broader advancement of knowledge and understanding.

References

Alferink, L. A., & Farmer−Dougan, V. (2010). Brain−(not) based education: Dangers of misunderstanding and misapplication of neuroscience research. *Exceptionality, 18*(1), 42−52.

Apple, M. (2001). Comparing neo−liberal projects and inequality in education. Comparative Education, 37(4), 409−423.

Athanases, S. Z., Banes, L. C., & Wong , J. W. (2015). Diverse language profiles: Leveraging resources of potential bilingual teachers of color. *Bilingual Research Journal, 38*(1), 65−87.

Athanases, S. & Wong, J. W. (2018). Learning from analyzing linguistically diverse students' work: A contribution of preservice teacher inquiry. *The Educational Forum, 82*(2), 191−207

Bacon, C. K. (2017). Multilanguage, multipurpose: A literature review, synthesis, and framework for critical literacies in English language teaching. *Journal of Literacy Research. 49*(3). 424−453.

Bartolome, L. (1994). Beyond the methods fetish: Toward a humanizing pedagogy. *Harvard Educational Review, 64*(2), 173−195.

Bartolome, L. I. (1996). Beyond the methods fetish: Toward a humanizing pedagogy. *Breaking free: The transformative power of critical pedagogy*, 229252.

Beauchamp, C. & Thomas, L. (2009). Understanding teacher identity: an overview of issues in the literature and implications for teacher education. *Cambridge Journal of Education, 39*(2), 175−189.

Butzkamm, W. (2011). Why make them crawl if they can walk? Teaching with mother tongue support. *RELC Journal, 42*(3), 379−391.

Canagarajah, S. & Ashraf, H. (2013).Multilingualism and education in South Asia: Resolving policy/practice dilemmas. Annual Review of Applied Linguistics, 33, 258

−285.

Cardona Moltó, M. C., Florian, L., Rouse, M. & Stough, L. M. (2010) Attitudes to diversity: a cross-cultural study of education students in Spain, England and the United States, *European Journal of Teacher Education, 33*(3), 245−264, DOI: 10.1080/02619768.2010.495771

Creswell, J. W. (2013). *Research design: Qualitative, quantitative, and mixed methods approaches.* SAGE Publications.

Creswell, J. W. (2015). *A concise introduction to mixed methods research.* SAGE Publications.

Creswell, J. W., & Poth, C. N. (2018). *Qualitative inquiry and research design: Choosing among five approaches.* SAGE Publications.

Dana, N. F., Yendol−Hoppey, D., & Snow−Gerono (2006). Deconstructing inquiry in the professional development school: Exploring the domains and contents of teachers' questions. *Action in Teacher Education, 27*(4), 59−71.

Daniel, S. M. (2014). Learning to educate English language learners in pre−service elementary practicums. *Teacher Education Quarterly, Spring* 2014, 5−28.

Daniel, S. M. & Pray, L. (2017). Learning to teach English language learners: A study of elementary school teachers' sense−making in an ELL endorsement program. *TESOL Quarterly, 51*(4), 787−819.

de Oliveira, L. C. (2016). A language−based approach to content instruction (LACI) for English language learners: Examples from two elementary teachers. *International Multilingual Research Journal. 10*(3), 217−231.

Denzin, N. K., & Lincoln, Y. S. (2017). *The SAGE Handbook of qualitative research* (5th ed.) SAGE Publications.

Dinham, J., Chalk, B., Beltman, S., Glass, C., & Nguyen, B. (2017). Pathways to resilience: how drawings reveal pre−service teachers' core narratives underpinning their future teacher−selves. *Asia−Pacific Journal of Teacher Education, 45*(2), 126−144.

Fang, Z., & Wang, Z. (2011). Beyond rubrics: Using functional language analysis to evaluate student writing. *Australian Journal of Language & Literacy, 34*(2), 147−165.

Golombek, P. & Doran, M. (2014). Unifying cognition, emotion, and activity in language teacher professional development. *Teaching and Teacher Education, 39*(2014), 102–111.

Gomez , M. L. , Rodriguez , T. L. , & Agosto , V. (2008). Life histories of Latino/a teacher candidates. *Teachers College Record, 110*(8), 1639 – 1676.

Harford, J. (2010). Teacher education policy in Ireland and the challenges of the twenty-first century. *European Journal of Teacher Education, 33*(4), 349–360.

Harvard Catalyst (2022). *Mixed methods research.* Harvard College. https://catalyst.harvard.edu/community–engagement/mmr/

Hawkey, K. (2006). Emotional intelligence and mentoring in pre–service teacher education: A literature review. *Mentoring & Tutoring. 14*(2), 137–147.

Hilliker, S. & Laletina, A. (2018). What do mainstream teachers think, know, and think they know about English language learners? NYS TESOL Journal, 5(1), 30–50.

Hoy, W. K., & Adams, C. M. (2016). *Quantitative research in education: A primer.* SAGE Publications.

Kavanagh, S. S. & Rainey, E. C. (2017). Learning to support adolescent literacy: Techer educator pedagogy and novice teacher take up in secondary English language arts teacher preparation. *American Educational Research Journal, 54*(5), 904–937.

Kim, H. J. (2021). Exploring three mainstream teacher candidates' professional identities and teachers of English language learners. [Unpublished doctoral dissertation]. University of Florida.

Lucas, T., Strom, K., Bratkovich, M., & Wnuk, J. (2018). Inservice preparation for mainstream teachers of English language learners: A review of the empirical literature. *The Educational Forum, 82*(2), 156–173.

Makalela, L. (2015). Translanguaging as a vehicle for epistemic access: Cases for reading comprehension and multilingual interactions. *Per Linguam: a Journal of Language Learning= Per Linguam: Tydskrif vir Taalaanleer, 31*(1), 15–29.

Narvaez Trejo, O. M. & Heffington, D. (2011). Exploring Teachers' Perceptions of their Role in the EFL Classroom: Some Considerations. *Memorias del VI foro de estudios en lenguas internacional* (FEL 2010). Retrieved from: http://www.uv.mx/personal/onarvaez/files/2012/09/Exploring−Teachers−percept ions−of−their−Role−in−the−EFL−Classroom.pdf

North, C. E. (2006). More than words? Delving into the substantive meaning (s) of "social justice" in education. *Review of Educational Research, 76*(4), 507−535.

Pugh, M. (2004). Peacekeeping and critical theory. *International peacekeeping, 11*(1), 39−58.

Pulitano, E. (2013). In liberty's shadow: the discourse of refugees and asylum seekers in critical race theory and immigration law/politics. *Identities, 20*(2), 172−189.

SAGE Research Methods (2022). *Methods map.* SAGE Publications. https://methods.sagepub.com/methods−map

Sahlberg, P. (2011). PISA in Finland: An education miracle or an obstacle to change?. *CEPS Journal: Center for Educational Policy Studies Journal, 1*(3), 119.

Shafiq, M. N. & Ross, K. (2010). Educational attainment and attitudes towards war in Muslim countries contemplating war: The cases of Jordan, Lebanon, Pakistan, and Turkey. *Journal of Development Studies, 46*(8), 1424−1441.

Short, D. J., Fidelman, C. G., & Louguit, M. (2012). Developing academic language in English language learners through sheltered instruction. *Tesol Quarterly, 46*(2), 334−361.

Villegas, A. M., SaizdeLaMora, K., Martin, A. D., & Mills, T. (2018). Preparing future mainstream teachers to teach English language learners: A review of the empirical literature. *The Educational Forum, 82*(2), 138−155.

Zeichner, K. (2010). Rethinking the connections between campus courses and field experiences in college− and university−based teacher education. *Journal of Teacher Education, 61*(1−2), 89−99.

Authors' Biography

Hyunjin Jinna Kim, Ph.D.

Hyunjin Jinna Kim is currently a Postdoctoral Associate at Stony Brook University. She previously taught English as a Foreign Language in South Korea for three years in a K−5 setting. She also taught English as a Second Language, academic composition, multicultural education, teaching methods and assessment, and teacher preparation practicum in higher education to undergraduate and graduate students for five years. She is interested in and has presented several professional development workshop sessions to teachers and postsecondary−level instructors to promote culturally and linguistically responsive pedagogy for diverse learners.

She earned her Bachelor's degree in Early Childhood Education from Ewha Womans University in South Korea. She received her M.A. in TESL (Teaching English as a Second Language) from the Pennsylvania State University and her Ph.D. in Curriculum and Instruction with ESOL/Bilingual Education specialization from the University of Florida.

Her research broadly focuses on the advocacy of marginalized populations and social justice education in various educational settings, including teacher education and preparation, PreK−12 education, and postsecondary education. She studies issues related to minoritized linguistic, cultural, ethnic, and racial identities in education and explores ways to provide equitable and inclusive education.

Yong−Jik Lee, Ph.D.

Yong−Jik earned his Bachelor's degree in English from Chung−Ang University in South Korea. He received his M.A. in TESL (Teaching English as a Second Language) from Indiana State University and his Ph.D. in Curriculum and Instruction with ESOL/Bilingual Education specialization from the University of Florida. His research broadly focuses on the teaching methods and educational technology in various educational settings, including teacher education and preparation. He was working with many international graduate students at a Korean university. He works as a Research Professor at Chonnam National University in South Korea.

A Handbook for Educational Research and Academic Writing
: From Idea to Reporting Your Research

Published the first edition in 2024. 1. 5

Author	Hyunjin Jinna Kim · Yong-Jik Lee
President	No Hyun
Publishing Company	Parkyoung Publishing & Company
	#210, 53, Gasan digital 2-ro, Geumcheon-gu, Seoul
	Registered in 2014.2.12. 2018−000080

tel	82-2-733-6771
fax	82-2-736-4818
e−mail	pys@pybook.co.kr
homepage	www.pybook.co.kr

ISBN	979-11-6519-492-5 93370

₩15,000